All Time High

All Time High

The Power of Cryptocurrencies
and How to Invest the Right Way

SYDEL SIERRA

Copyright © Sydel Sierra 2024
First published by the kind press 2024

The moral right of the author to be identified as the author of this work has been asserted.

All rights reserved. Without limiting the rights under copyright reserved above, no part of this publication may be reproduced, stored in or introduced into a retrieval system, or transmitted, in any form or by any means (electronic, mechanical, photocopying, recording or otherwise) without the prior written permission of the publisher of this book.

A catalogue record for this book is available from the National Library of Australia.

Paperback ISBN: 978-0-6458993-4-4
eBook ISBN: 978-0-6458993-5-1

Print information available on the last page.

We at The Kind Press acknowledge that Aboriginal and Torres Strait Islander peoples are the Traditional Custodians and the first storytellers of the lands on which we live and work; and we pay our respects to Elders past and present.

THE KIND PRESS

www.thekindpress.com

While the publisher and author have used their best efforts in preparing this book, they make no representations or warranties with respect to the accuracy or completeness of the contents of this book and specifically disclaim any implied warranties of merchantability or fitness for a particular purpose. The advice and strategies contained in this book may not be suitable for your situation. You should consult with a professional where appropriate. We advise that the information contained in this book does not negate personal responsibility on the part of the reader for their own wealth, health or safety. Neither the publisher nor author shall be liable for any loss of profit or any other commercial damages, including but not limited to special, incidental, consequential, or other damages.

Contents

Introduction	xiii
Why I Wrote This Book	xvi
My Story	xviii

PART ONE
The Big Opportunity With Crypto

Chapter 1	Can Someone Tell Me What Crypto Actually Is?	1
	What We Have Now	4
	The Plan B of Currency	5
Chapter 2	The Problems Crypto Solves	8
Chapter 3	Top Crypto Fears and How to Break Free of Them	11
	Fear #1 I'll Be Scammed and Lose All My Money	12
	Fear #2 Crypto Is for Techy People Only	13
	Fear #3 I Missed All the Big Profits	14
	Fear #4 I'm Uncomfortable with Becoming My Own Bank	15
	Fear #5 Crypto Is Just Too Volatile and Overwhelming for Me	17
	Fear #6 Crypto Is Just a Fad	19
Chapter 4	The Real Opportunity with Crypto	26
	Life-Changing Gains of 10x, 100x, Even 10,000x	26
	An Early Retirement	28
	An Equal Playing Field	29
	A Consistent Passive Income of $500-$1,500 Extra Per Week	30
	The Same Opportunity as the Internet? The Internet 2.0!	31
	Freedom to Live Life on Your Terms	32
	Seeing the Big Picture	33
Chapter 5	Bullish Catalysts That Will Drive Market Prices	34

	Bullish Catalyst 1: The Economy Skating on Thin Ice	35
	Bullish Catalyst 2: The Greatest Wealth Transfer in History is About to Happen	38
	Bullish Catalyst 3: Wall Street's Greed	43
	Bullish Catalyst 4: Every Four Years … This Happens	45
Chapter 6	When Opportunity Knocks, Will You Answer?	52

PART TWO
Key Crypto Investing Secrets

Chapter 7	The Difference Between a Bull Market and a Bear Market	62
Chapter 8	Delay Gratification, Create Financial Freedom	65
Chapter 9	Balance Your Emotions, Increase Your Gains	67
Chapter 10	Industry Tools to Navigate Crypto Markets	71
Chapter 11	Bitcoin Is Your Key Indicator	75
Chapter 12	Super Cycles: Look to the Past, to Know the Future	77
Chapter 13	How to Time Your Entry Like a Pro	87
	Zone 1: Accumulation – The Pessimism Zone	88
	Zone 2: Preparation – Market Starts to Move	89
	Zone 3: Bull Market – Market Is Running Hot	90
	Zone 4: Bear Market – Prices Are Dropping	91
Chapter 14	Inside a Bull Market	95
	Key Event 1: Bitcoin Leads the Way	95
	Key Event 2: Ethereum's Turn	96
	Key Event 3: Large Cap Cryptos Step In	96
	Key Event 4: Small Cap Meme Season Marks the Near End	96
Chapter 15	Crypto Investing: It's a Plan, Within a Plan, Within a Plan	98

PART THREE
Create Your Portfolio And Make It Work For You

Chapter 16	Private Keys and the Golden Rule of Crypto	108
	Tip #1 Never Take a Photo of Your Private Keys	109
	Tip #2 Store Your Keys Offline	109
	Tip #3 Test Your Seed Phrase	110

Chapter 17	Crypto Wallets and Storing Your Digital Wealth	113
Chapter 18	Choosing the Right Exchange to Buy Your Crypto	116
Chapter 19	Create Your First Portfolio	121
	Step 1: Ask These Questions	122
	Step 2: Do You Know Your Actual Risk Tolerance?	125
	Step 3: How Many Coins Will You Hold?	127
	Step 4: Deploy Your Cash	129
	Step 5: Look for Major Growth Sectors	131
	Step 6: Create a Winning Portfolio	138
Chapter 20	Frustration Breeds Opportunities	142
Chapter 21	Make Your Portfolio Work for You	144
	Will You Be Defensive or Aggressive?	147
	Stakes Are Like Businesses	147
Chapter 22	The Biggest Mistakes New Crypto Investors Make	150
Chapter 23	Are You Ready?	157

PART FOUR
Take Profit And Unlock Financial Freedom

Chapter 24	A Lesson in History	165
Chapter 25	Profit Taking Is Vision Creating	168
Chapter 26	No One Has a Perfect Sell Record	171
Chapter 27	Selling Strategies and Concepts	173
Chapter 28	How Will You Sell?	183
Chapter 29	Unlocking Freedom	187

PART FIVE
Elevate Your Mindset, Master Your Life

Chapter 30	The Crypto Surprise	197
Chapter 31	What Are Your Stories?	199
Chapter 32	How Do You Spend Your Time?	201
Chapter 33	Unpacking Your Aversion to Wealth	203
Chapter 34	Becoming At Ease with Wealth	206
Chapter 35	We Live in a Consent-Based Realm	210

Chapter 36	Every Action in Crypto Places You a Step Ahead	213
Chapter 37	Don't Wait for Crypto to Grab You	215
Chapter 38	When Rules No Longer Apply	216
A Final Note: How to Cash In on the Big Opportunity Happening Right Now		218

Get Started with Digital Wealth Group	*220*
About Your Author	*221*
A Message of Gratitude	*222*
Notes	*224*

Introduction

We stand on the precipice of extraordinary transformation!

What if I told you that we're at the beginning of a paradigm shift that will change every aspect of our lives? That the world of crypto and blockchain technology is not only here to stay, but also set to become the most disruptive force we'll see in our lifetime? The fascinating world of crypto cannot be stopped, and it's set to make more millionaires than any other asset before it. I truly believe investing in crypto has the potential to offer complete financial freedom and life-changing wealth you can retire on. And I'm not talking about twenty or thirty years' time either ... I'm talking about the next few years.

How do I know this?

Because I've done it. And I've helped many others do it too.

When I first started on my crypto journey, it was a no-man's-land and information was like gold dust. I spent hours attending local crypto gatherings and scouring the Internet for any piece of information we could find! Fast forward to today, and the opposite is true—we're overwhelmed with info, and the negative voices can often be the loudest.

We've all heard the stories about crypto being a scam, a Ponzi scheme or used for illegal activities. Or perhaps you've heard the best gains are over and there's no way you can profit from it now. These narratives keep us stuck in fear, sitting on the sidelines and missing one of the greatest financial opportunities of our lifetime.

The truth is, crypto is not just for tech-savvy traders who spend their days analysing charts and decoding algorithms. While this may have been the case once upon a time, it's far from the reality today. Why? Because crypto is on the verge of mainstream global adoption. And today, your average crypto investor could be a couple with kids, grey nomads on their retirement adventure, or a schoolteacher setting herself up for financial success. One of the true gifts of crypto is its ability to break down traditional barriers and level the playing field. Crypto is not an exclusive playground for a few techy developers, it's an inclusive space that is there for everyone.

I hear from so many people who are curious about getting into crypto, but they're hesitant to take the first step. They may have achieved success in other areas of their lives, but they've put a block up between themselves and the crypto world. And I get it. At first glance it seems overwhelming. But when we break it down, piece by piece, I guarantee this will be one of the most enjoyable and lucrative journeys you embark on. One of the best things about what I do is being able to share what I've learned and inspire others to grow their knowledge, wealth and power.

At its heart, crypto is a tool for empowerment. It's not about conforming to a stereotype; it's about breaking free from financial constraints. So, I invite you to drop your perceptions of what a crypto investor looks like and give yourself the opportunity to experience the life-changing wealth that crypto can create. I invite you, with this book, to see how simple it really can be. By following my methods, you can experience a safe entry into the world of crypto that has been proven to help thousands of people since 2017.

Within these pages you'll find:

- A down-to-earth explanation of what crypto is, why it's here to stay and the big opportunity it presents for each and every one of us.
- The problems crypto solves and why it's set to revolutionise our world.
- Easy to understand instructions for how you, too, can profit from the fastest appreciating asset class of all time.
- The methods and concepts I teach to disintegrate limiting beliefs around money and financial freedom.
- A demonstration of safe investing strategies that any new investor, regardless of age, background or education level, can benefit from.

I've been saying for years that a currency crisis is coming. The old systems are on their way out, and faster, fairer and more sophisticated technologies are taking their place. Those who smartly position themselves now will have the best opportunity to reap the rewards. With this book, you'll learn the skills to confidently participate in the biggest wealth transfer of our lifetime.

So, I invite you to join me and learn about this incredible asset class. It's time to carve out your path to true wealth and financial freedom—forever! Let's build you a safe and highly successful cryptocurrency portfolio so you can truly live the life of your dreams.

Why I Wrote This Book

When I was starting out in crypto, I spent half of my time confused and the other half completely overwhelmed. I thought of crypto as a male-dominated world and I was constantly questioning my place in it. But as I persevered and dived deeper into all the problems that crypto solves, I moved out of overwhelm and into excitement! And that excitement skyrocketed once I took my first profits.

I still remember the day my initial investment of $3,000 reached $30,000. The feeling of pride and accomplishment was amazing! But when I turned $30,000 into $300,000 and $300,000 into multiple millions, that feeling became indescribable. Why? Because I'd proven to myself that I could. I took the time to learn something new, apply it in a world that was unfamiliar to me and reach an unprecedented level of success. Despite the voice in my head telling me I didn't belong here, I continued to educate myself about crypto, and my determination rewarded me time and time again. As I built out my portfolio and learned more about cycles and patterns, that initial hesitancy dissolved and I saw that building wealth didn't have to be daunting or intimidating at all. It was exciting and invigorating and quite easy to do. This is what crypto gave to me, and this is what I want other investors to experience as well—a sense of accomplishment and achievement in knowing you can master your financial world.

The reality for so many people is that we hold trauma stories around money. We carry limiting beliefs that tell us it's too hard to learn anything new, we're not smart enough to invest, we're too old or we might make a mistake and lose whatever money we could gain. These beliefs lead to one place only—limitation. With this book, I encourage you to step out of those shackles and into a world of financial opportunity, growth and abundance. This journey is about building your confidence as much as it is about building your wealth and I assure you, the milestones you reach here will motivate you in all areas of life.

Crypto has given me a remarkable gift, one that I aspire for all new investors to share—a sense of accomplishment and achievement within the realm of finance. I've experienced a deep transformation in my own life, and I've witnessed it in the lives of the students I've guided. I invite you to see what crypto has to offer and share this knowledge with your family and friends.

So, get ready to unlock those fears, break free from the traditional financial norms, and embrace the power of crypto. It's not just about money; it's about owning your financial narrative and creating a life you desire. Join me on a journey of education, empowerment and opportunity.

There's never been a better time than right now.

My Story

My career as a crypto educator started very organically, and quite by chance.

I first heard the words 'Bitcoin' and 'Cryptocurrencies' in 2016. I was in a business workshop in Northern Europe with a number of entrepreneurs and creative business leaders. Some individuals in the room were making purchase orders for thousands of Bitcoin at a time.

I wondered what they knew that I didn't.

These investors spoke passionately about a new currency that was going to change the world. I remember hearing the phrase 'the writing is on the wall' multiple times as they talked about the financial system and the failures that would inevitably occur. They talked about major gains and institutional involvement in crypto before it was even a thing.

And you know what? They were right.

At the time, I was building a martial arts empire with my family in Australia, and we became known as one of the largest martial arts schools during that time. We had over fifty instructors and a student base of hundreds of members. We travelled back and forth to China, Malaysia and Singapore and were even inducted into the Hall of Fame in Kuala Lumpur. It was a busy, fulfilling and satisfying venture, but there was something I just couldn't get out of my head ...

The idea of financial freedom and sovereignty.

Like so many others, I was in a cycle of swapping my hours for dollars. And even though I enjoyed my work, I couldn't shake the idea that there had to be another way. The concept of financial freedom captured my imagination and I found myself wondering if such a thing was possible. Could I create a life that was entirely on my terms? Or was that a reality reserved for only a lucky few?

At the same time all this was happening, my brother, Aden, was working in the mines in north Western Australia. Like many miners, he was isolated from family and friends for weeks and months at a time. The pay was great, but so were the demands of the job and the sacrifices it required. They call it 'golden handcuffs' because it's gruelling work, but the pay is often too good to leave. It's no surprise that he, too, was questioning the predicament he found himself in. He was also thinking *'there must be a better way'*.

That's when we discovered crypto.

Coincidentally, we came to crypto at the same time. So, we joined forces to learn everything we could about this emerging new asset class.

Was this information easy to find? Absolutely not. We were in a landscape where knowledge was scarce and guidance was non-existent. Our only point of contact was a friend who'd been mining Bitcoin since 2009 (and earning fifty Bitcoin every ten minutes). He knew the basics of buying and storing Bitcoin, but this was just the tip of the iceberg in terms of cryptocurrencies.

So, we did what any inspired, motivated or curious person would do—we threw ourselves into learning everything we could about crypto. We dedicated ourselves to crypto meetups, Internet forums, and hours of online research so that in early 2017, we were ready to make our first purchase. We turned a very modest investment into a significant profit. How significant am I talking? Well, one of our coin picks, NEO, went from a $983 USD dollar investment to over $108,790 USD in ninety days—a 10,879% gain. At the time, this was equivalent to 26.8 Bitcoin (around $106,000 USD at the time).

Needless to say, the gains from NEO and several other crypto coins were enough for us to turn our focus entirely to cryptocurrencies, and the people around us wanted to know how we did it. We started teaching our family and friends and before we knew it, we were doing the rounds of everyone we knew. We'd show up at their houses, set up their crypto wallets, show them how to buy coins safely and demonstrate the process so they could do it themselves. They told their friends, who told their friends, and soon we were running weekend workshops to show everyone how to get started.

We had a system that was simple, safe and consistently generated profits.

Our friends and family began to make money by following our guidelines, and so began the start of our legacy and one of the most enriching experiences of my life.

The Unexpected Global Take Off

There we were, my brother and I, educating everyone we knew about this amazing way to create wealth, when we received an interesting phone call. We were asked to present to a room of sixty investors about cryptocurrencies.

The catch? We had to create twelve, sixty-minute presentations from scratch. In less than a week.

To say it was challenging was an understatement. But despite the late nights and early mornings leading up to it, the success of that event in early 2018 laid the foundation for global growth and created the Digital Wealth Group (DWG) that exists today. From that one event, we began travelling around Australia and overseas to educate people on cryptocurrencies. We spoke in front of thousands about our system to get into crypto the safe way and the right way. We demonstrated the simple strategies we used to position ourselves for generational wealth, as well as the big opportunity that cryptocurrencies presented.

We shared the stage with the likes of Robert Kiyosaki, Harry Dent, John Di Martini and many other well-known figures of the financial and personal development world. You simply couldn't stop us. In those days, I was practically living out of a suitcase and the airport felt like my second home. The weeks were a blur of cities, stages and destinations, but it was all worth it because we had a powerful message to deliver.

The importance of self-sovereignty and financial freedom.

In under two years, my brother and I had built a reputation as the leading educators in crypto. But not only that, we were one of the very first companies to offer one-to-one private coaching, where you could have a trusted advisor take you through every step of the investing process. It's been a remarkable journey, and the growth continues to this day. In fact, we have a goal to help over 30,000 families become financially free and we are well on our way to achieving it.

From humble beginnings, we've created a global network of people who are taking ownership over their finances, expanding their mindset, planting seeds of greatness for the future and creating wealth for themselves and their families. But more than that, our community is invested in true sovereignty and freedom for everyone. It's about creating a better humanity, where we are all free of fear narratives, free of restrictions, free to be who we truly are.

PART ONE

The Big Opportunity With Crypto

Key Terms & Translations

In this section we talk about:

Blockchain: A *very* fancy spreadsheet that can never be altered and is visible to everyone.
Decentralization: Peer to peer, no middleman.
HODL: Slang for 'Hold On for Dear Life' (a humorous term to describe the volatility).
FOMO: Slang for 'Fear of Missing Out'.
Crypto Trader: An investor who trades the market daily, weekly and/or monthly.
Crypto Investor: Buy and hold, longer term investor.
Retail Investor: Your everyday investor e.g. Next-door neighbour, boss, friend, aunty.
Institutional Investor: Traditional finance and accredited investors.
Volatility: The price changes within the market.
Gains: Measured in percent growth or dollars earnt on a particular cryptocurrency.
Asymmetric Opportunity: For every $1 you invest, you have the opportunity to make $10 or more.
Private Keys / Seed Phrase / Keys: A collection of words that act as the key to your crypto.
Staking: Similar to a term deposit except you lock up your crypto and get paid interest for it.
Sovereign: Possessing complete authority over your own life.

Chapter 1

Can Someone Tell Me What Crypto Actually Is?

"Bitcoin is a remarkable cryptographic achievement and the ability to create something which is not duplicable in the digital world has enormous value."
Eric Schmidt, Former CEO of Google

In its most basic terms, cryptocurrency is digital money that you, and only you, have control of.

Crypto was built on the premise of self-sovereignty and personal ownership, in other words—owning your financial destiny. No banks, no financial institutions and no advisors in suits telling you what to do! For the first time ever, you have the keys to the financial kingdom and the means to build immense wealth for generations to come. In short, cryptocurrency is a game changer.

How can this be? Well, it all comes down to blockchain technology and decentralisation.

You see, cryptocurrency plus blockchain technology equals digital trust. And in a world where we are increasingly digital, the value proposition for this is enormous.

So, what is a blockchain? It's essentially a digital ledger or record-keeping system maintained by a network of people all around the world. The decentralised nature of blockchains makes it very hard to tamper with the information because once something is added to the blockchain, it can't be changed, reversed, edited or deleted without permission and consensus from *all* involved. In fact, while blockchain technology was originally created for crypto, the security and transparency mean it can be used for anything that requires trust, from tracking within supply chains to preventing fraud to recording votes in elections. The blockchain is online, available to anyone with an Internet connection, and you can check on any transaction, anywhere around the world, from the beginning of time. Can you think of any bank that is as openly transparent as this?

To understand cryptocurrencies better, let's take a look at our traditional financial system.

What We Have Now

If you've ever tried asking someone about our monetary system, you'll receive a mixed bag of responses, from knowledge, to avoidance, to complete indifference. This comes down to two things:

1. Our monetary system floats on a sea of political and financial jargon, deterring people from understanding the mess it actually is.
2. People simply don't think about where money comes from, as long as they receive their pay and can afford their lifestyle (something which is increasingly harder to do).

So, if people don't particularly care, why do we even need an alternative monetary system? Quite simply because our current system is on the verge of collapse.

You see, when we stopped using the international gold standard, we switched from a physical commodity that has tangible value to fiat money, which is government-issued and not backed by a physical commodity. Unlike gold, fiat has no intrinsic value. It's essentially a promise that the currency is worth something and can be exchanged for goods. In other words, it's valuable because we believe the issuing government when they say, 'Hey, this piece of paper is worth something'. It's essentially backed by the faith of the bearer, and nothing more. Fiat money gives governments full control of its supply and value, and they use this power to stabilise the economy and global markets. But there are many problems with this. Fiat money is slow, expensive and outdated. It's not a scarce or fixed resource like gold is, so governments can print more whenever they choose. And what happens if they print too much? Boom, the value takes a nosedive and suddenly your coffee costs a small fortune.

So, with every new dollar printed, year in and year out, the value of our hard-earned cash gets diluted, and the purchasing power of our dollar is diminished. This sets an alarming precedent. When governments have this much control over our assets, we need to have a plan B.

Enter, the superhero of the financial world, Bitcoin.

The Plan B of Currency

Bitcoin was launched in 2009 as a response to the 2008 financial crisis, which revealed huge problems with our fiat-based system. The aim was to establish a decentralised, peer-to-peer electronic currency that would give ordinary people control over their finances and remove centralised banks and financial institutions from the equation.

Translation: To remove the middleman.

Bitcoin wasn't just looking to be a digital currency, it aimed to be the *people's* currency. A way for anyone with an Internet connection and a device to take control of their financial destiny. Bitcoin could be owned by anyone in the world, and transactions were fast, secure, borderless and cheap. How cheap? Well, in 2019 a whopping $512 million worth of Bitcoin was transferred from one wallet to another in less than three minutes. The cost? Less than $3.

Try doing that with your regular bank and see how much you're left with.

Bitcoin is often referred to as gold for the Internet age, or 'digital gold' because it has a capped supply. It can't be conjured out of thin air like fiat currency can. It's programmed to be scarce, thanks to a process called the *Bitcoin Halving* (more about this later) that keeps inflation at bay.

But here's where it gets even better: there's a maximum supply of 21 million Bitcoins in the world. After April 2024, based on the circulating supply and a techy term called the 'stock to flow ratio', Bitcoin is the scarcest asset in the world, even above gold. In fact, the scarcity of Bitcoin supersedes gold because Bitcoin is ruled by an immutable code. Once the last Bitcoin has been mined and the supply is exhausted, that's it, there is no more that can be 'discovered' from anywhere. Code cannot be tampered with or changed. Code is law.

Bitcoin's journey has been nothing short of remarkable. It's evolved from a speculative curiosity to a force that has won hearts, gained trust, and increased in value immensely. It's even gained traction with the large institutional investors who were initially calling it a scam! So, the same entities that once scorned it now seek to leverage its potential for their organisation.

In 2009, the game changed forever. The launch of Bitcoin enabled a brand-new way of transacting, paving the way for the plethora of cryptocurrencies we have today. In the not-too-distant future, we'll be able to transact in digital currency for everything—from our morning coffee to our dream property purchase. What lies ahead is a momentous shift—an inevitable surge in global adoption, not just among retail investors (everyday people), but at the institutional level too. The infrastructure is rapidly evolving and becoming more sophisticated, ready to embrace these industry giants and the capital they bring. It's not a matter of 'if' wide scale institutional adoption will occur, it's simply a matter of when. And as the titans of the financial world enter the crypto space, the stage is set for a monumental paradigm shift.

So, I ask you, which side of the institutional wave do you want to be on?

This is the power of knowing what's coming and positioning ourselves accordingly.

Chapter 2

The Problems Crypto Solves

Never before has our financial system been disrupted to such an enormous scale. And ...
We are only at the beginning.

So now you know a bit about why Bitcoin was created, let's talk about the problems that Bitcoin and other cryptocurrencies solve.

Currently in our fiat money system, we have a central body, such as a bank or financial institution, looking after our funds. This comes with certain safeguards, but it also comes with restrictions. For instance, we can only access small amounts of our money at a time, we need permission to do certain things, and in extreme cases, we can be locked out of our own accounts. Dealing with banks requires lengthy application and assessment processes and constantly having to validate our identity to do the simplest of tasks.

Exhausting!

Cryptocurrency, on the other hand, has no one gatekeeping your funds but you. It can't be shut down like a centralised system can and it's not subject to the rules, regulations or whims of one controlling authority. Crypto takes the middleman out of the equation and gives full power and custody of your money back to you.

Crypto tackles some of the key inefficiencies and vulnerabilities that have plagued our financial system for so long. When you think about it, the world has moved on in so many ways, yet we persist in a problematic currency that is slow and outdated. It's like an old clunky computer struggling to keep up with the sleek, efficient laptops of today. We need a complete overhaul of our monetary system and crypto is that solution. With crypto, we get:

Reduced Costs: Whether you're sending pocket change to your next-door neighbour or a million dollars half-way across the world, crypto transactions are significantly cheaper in every aspect.

Financial Inclusion: Anyone with an Internet connection and a wallet can participate and transact with their crypto.

Accessible Global Markets: Crypto markets are open twenty-four/seven, allowing anyone to trade and invest at any time, from anywhere.

Cross-Border Transactions: Ever transferred money across borders and thought a message in a bottle would get there quicker? Well, crypto flips that entirely. Where traditional cross-border transactions are slow, pricey and subject to intermediaries, crypto is fast and direct.

Inflation Resistance: Many cryptocurrencies have capped supplies, making them resistant to the inflationary pressures that erode the value of fiat money. No more watching your hard-earned cash lose its value over time.

Transparency: The blockchain is like a truth serum for transactions. It's transparent and immutable, meaning once it's there, it's there for good, reducing fraud and corruption.

Zero Censorship: With crypto and private ownership, you're captain of your financial ship. Your funds can't be seized, frozen, or controlled by third parties if you make a lifestyle choice that they don't like.

So, as you can see, crypto is a realm where costs shrink, borders vanish and financial power is in the hands of the many, not the few. It provides us with the opportunity to take the power back for ourselves.

And what comes with great power? Great responsibility!

Up until now, we've been entrusting our hard-earned money and investments to third party entities to look after. Crypto is a little different. It requires us to step into full responsibility for our finances, something which can seem daunting to start with, but I assure you, the opportunity, sense of empowerment and potential for life-changing returns is 100% worth it.

As a new investor, you no doubt have some fears or hesitations around crypto, so in the next chapter I'll address the key fears I hear time and time again when it comes to this revolutionary asset class.

Chapter 3

Top Crypto Fears and How to Break Free of Them

Those who are solely guided by fear in this market miss the huge opportunity that research and informed decisions can unlock.

So now you know what crypto is and the problems it solves, let's talk about some of the reasons new investors might fear it. And trust me when I say I've heard it all! Most of the time, these fears are powered by one of two things:

1. A lack of education about crypto
2. An ignorance toward this asset class and what it's capable of

In both cases, these fears can have new investors sitting on the sidelines and missing out on one of the greatest opportunities for early retirement and financial freedom for themselves and their families.

So, let's address the key fears I hear time and time again.

Fear #1
I'll Be Scammed and Lose All My Money

This is probably one of the biggest hurdles for people entering into crypto, and I don't blame anyone for feeling this way. Media loves to spin narratives and gives prominence to fear-generating news around hacks, scams and fraud. While it's true that there are pitfalls in cryptocurrency, it's also quite easy to avoid them altogether. I guarantee that with some basic knowledge, you'll see how easy it is to keep your crypto assets safe. This is the only way I teach crypto—the safe way.

Digital Wealth Group students are considered to have the safest practices in the world because I teach the importance of private custody, owning your own crypto and keeping it in a wallet that you control at *all* times. This means getting your funds off the exchanges as soon as possible. I will explain exactly how this all works later, but it's a crucial piece of information you'll need to know when you start buying crypto.

The other golden rule that will keep your crypto assets safe is that you should never, ever reveal your private keys under any circumstances. When you're the sole guardian of those keys, you're in total control and you can safeguard your assets like a pro. Scammers will try to extract your keys off you, but you never, ever need to share them.

When you apply my security protocols, which I discuss later, you can easily keep the scammers out, and keep your treasures safe, secure and locked up tight.

Fear #2
Crypto Is for Techy People Only

A common misconception in the crypto world is that it's reserved for tech-savvy people and trading gurus only. Allow me to set the record straight once and for all: it's simply not true.

Thinking that crypto is too techy is like saying you can't drive a car because you're not a mechanic. Sure, the technology behind crypto can seem complicated at first, but its practical application is more user-friendly than you might think. This is not some closed-off world for developers; it's a universal playground for anyone with a bit of curiosity.

"You don't need to know everything about Crypto to be successful. You just need to know enough of the important bits."

Coach Michael, Digital Wealth Group

One of the elements that puts people off crypto is the jargon. HODL, FOMO, blockchain, NFTs—it sounds like a secret code, right? But every new thing comes with its lingo, and crypto is no different. Remember when emojis were the mysterious hieroglyphics of texting? Now, we use them without even thinking about it. Crypto is simply another language and, once you understand the foundations, it will start to flow much easier.

The other misconception is that you have to be a seasoned trader to take part. People often conflate trading with investing, but they're actually very different.

Trading is a strategy with higher stakes and greater risks and in my opinion is not for a beginner. That's why many seasoned investors will steer new crypto investors away from trading altogether. It demands more technical expertise and market knowledge to be able to react swiftly. Investing, on the other hand, is about long-term wealth accumulation and you don't necessarily need trading knowledge, just an interest in the coin you are investing into and an understanding of market cycles and sentiment. This is the strategy I teach, where investors can hold assets for months and years because we're less concerned with short-term price fluctuations. We know the long-term goal.

I think of cryptocurrency as the next progression in our financial evolution. We've all learned to embrace mobile apps, online banking and other advances that have made our lives easier. Navigating the terms and technology of crypto is similar, so never think it's beyond your reach.

At its core, crypto is about democratising finance. It offers financial inclusivity, opportunity and control to anyone with an Internet connection. So, the big question is, can you profit from this incredible asset class without a tech background?

The answer is, absolutely!

Fear #3
I Missed All the Big Profits

So many people believe it's too late to make money from crypto, and that if you didn't get in on Bitcoin and Ethereum at the start, you've already missed the boat. I'm constantly asked if the ship has sailed on crypto, and my answer is this:

Not only has the ship not sailed, it hasn't even finished being built!

Yes, Bitcoin and Ethereum have been through huge growth cycles and seen large profits, but there are cryptocurrencies coming to market all the time that are improving on that existing infrastructure and offering far greater gains than the original two. Bitcoin and Ethereum may have been the pioneers, but what's coming behind them will absolutely change the game.

In other words. The Apples and Amazons of the crypto world are yet to emerge.

It would be ludicrous to think that the largest gains and biggest opportunities have already happened in this space. Why? Well, just consider the evolution of the Internet. How many investment opportunities did the dotcom boom present, and did they all happen in the first few years? Absolutely not. The Internet continued to evolve and birth new innovations, platforms, and business models well beyond the dotcom boom. Crypto is no different, and its journey is just getting started. The potential for disruptive technologies and novel use cases extends far beyond what we've seen so far. Just as the Internet's potential wasn't fully realised in its early days, the power of blockchain technology is still unfolding. Crypto will present many ground-breaking opportunities that could create life-changing wealth for those who are willing to explore, research and invest wisely.

Fear #4
I'm Uncomfortable with Becoming My Own Bank

When we've become so used to big institutions controlling our money, some people find it daunting to think about taking full responsibility for it. After all, it's been this way for as long as we can remember, and many still want the perceived protection of a financial institution.

But here's the thing: true financial freedom and self-sovereignty can only occur when we embrace full responsibility.

Banks have played an undeniable role in our financial landscape for centuries. They've delivered a service we've all used, and we've benefitted from the convenience of someone else taking care of our money. However, in light of bank runs, forced bank closures and imposed restrictions, it's becoming increasingly clear that we need a plan B.

Is it the system's fault? Not quite. Banks only exist because we, as a society, created the need for them. At some point in time, we collectively chose to relinquish control over our finances and hand that burden onto someone else.

In short, we handed over the responsibility.

This pattern echoes across many monopolised industries today. Just think of how often we delegate and outsource responsibility in our lives, from industries like big pharma, right down to the food we eat. These entities thrive because we, as a society, want someone else to 'do it for us'. Many view this as how the world is. But it doesn't have to stay that way.

So, when we talk about true financial freedom, we have to recognise our role in creating these systems, then choose to take a more empowered stance. By educating yourself and using smart investing and storage methods you can ensure your wealth is always safeguarded. True responsibility can seem intimidating to start with, but it's far from the dangerous force we've been led to believe. It's a responsibility worth embracing—a call to reassess our role in these structures and choose a better, more sovereign path.

Fear #5
Crypto Is Just Too Volatile and Overwhelming for Me

I'm going to share a secret with you ... even the most experienced crypto traders and investors have moments of overwhelm. It's very much a shared experience in the crypto community.

But here's the thing about overwhelm. *On the other side of it lies the opportunity.*

When you first dip your toes into the world of crypto currencies, the sheer number of coins, exchanges, and technical jargon can leave your head spinning. But that sensation is a sign that you're onto something truly transformative. If it wasn't challenging or disruptive, how could it be called evolution? Any new technology and innovation has to first exist in a world where it is originally misunderstood. When something is new, it offers opportunity, and crypto brings many opportunities for us to capitalise on.

My suggestion. Embrace the overwhelm as a part of the learning journey and know that everyone has been through it at some point or another. Take things at your pace, don't push yourself, and don't beat yourself up if something is hard to grasp. Learning the ins and outs of this world is not an overnight process, but eventually things will start to click. There's an expression I use that sums this up beautifully.

The more you give to crypto, the more it will give to you.

Consider crypto education as an investment in itself. Read books, follow industry news, join online communities and seek advice from experienced crypto enthusiasts. The time you invest learning will pay dividends in the future and allow you to make well-informed investment choices, rather than following the fear and euphoria of the public. So, embrace the learning process, make confusion your friend, and turn crypto overwhelm into an opportunity for financial growth.

Which brings me to the volatility!

Many people take a quick look at crypto, see how volatile it is, then call it a day. They would rather wait until it's completely mainstream before taking the plunge and embracing crypto. But while these people sit on the sidelines, they're missing out on the opportunity for incredible early gains and life-changing wealth. Volatility is one of the defining characteristics of the crypto market and, contrary to popular belief, it's one of the most powerful tools for wealth creation. Particularly when you learn about market cycles and market psychology, which we cover later in the book.

At first glance, this space can seem like a chaotic Wild West, but the crypto market always plays out in cycles, and they're actually very predictable. Understanding these cycles and the key entry points will drastically impact your results with crypto and the performance of your portfolio. And trust me when I say the strategies are very simple.

The truth is, volatility is the price we pay for gains and there is currently no other asset class in the world that matches the gains you can achieve in the crypto market. So don't be afraid of the volatility. Turn it into a tool rather than a fear, because mastering this concept will drastically improve your results with every major market cycle.

Fear #6
Crypto Is Just a Fad

To address this fear, I'm going to reference three of the most well-known 'fads' in our history: automobiles, electricity and the Internet. Yes, once upon a time, these ground-breaking innovations were labelled fads. In fact, they were heavily criticised and feared. So, let's take a closer look at these disruptive technologies, and what they had to go through before they radically changed the way we live today.

Automobiles: The Very First Red Flag

What many people don't know is that the humble automobile was not only heavily criticised, it was denounced by the public when it was first introduced in the late 1800s. People were so frightened of it, they introduced a new law called the Red Flag Act in 1865. Under this law, anyone who purchased an automobile had to have three people operating it at any one time. The first was the operator, the second was an engineer and the third was to walk fifty metres in front, waving a red flag to warn people that a death machine was making its way down the track!

Source: Daimler

It seems ridiculous now, doesn't it? But back then, crowds would gather and watch as these cars passed by, struggling to drive on cobblestones, muddy surfaces and horse ruts. They couldn't effectively demonstrate the capabilities of the first cars because the infrastructure for cars hadn't been built. The road was designed for horses, and horses only.

So, the value proposition of the automobile, its capabilities and utility, were being demonstrated on the infrastructure for the technology (horse and cart) that it was trying to replace.

In the late 1800s people said:

"The horse is here to stay, but the automobile is only a novelty, a fad."

"How can you go anywhere with one fuel station in town?"

"Who would drive a loud machine that constantly breaks down?"

In short, the automobile was a laughingstock. But fast forward one-hundred years and many people have forgotten it was once like this. These days we have the infrastructure in place for cars, trains and all types of transport that we rely on.

Electricity: An Incredibly Dangerous Mystery Technology

Now let's go back in time to the late 1800s to mid-1900s. Electricity was the word on everyone's lips, and the people were terrified.

Why? Because fear-mongering in the newspapers was rife. Rather than celebrate the innovation, the papers showed photos of houses burning after failed electricity attempts. They ridiculed Nikola Tesla, the scientist who created Alternating Current (AC), and always portrayed him in the same way—sitting in highly conductive rooms while electricity was shooting from one side of the room to another. With all this going on, it's no wonder people were sceptical of this mysterious new technology. They didn't understand it when it was first introduced and were afraid of the disruption it was causing.

Another reason electricity was criticised is because people were satisfied with what they already had, which was gas-powered heating and lighting. Back then people were employed to walk the streets each night lighting the lamps that were fuelled by gas. Those who were wealthy enough could have gas lines running directly into their homes for interior heating.

So, when electricity was introduced, people were quick to say:

"What can electricity do that gas cannot?"

"Who would put lightning down their walls unless they want their house to catch on fire?"

"Electricity is just a fad."

Fast forward one-hundred years and again, things are very different. We have efficient lighting and heating. We have motors, air-conditioning, telecommunications, electronics and thousands of applications that now use and rely on electricity.

Now let's look at one of the most groundbreaking inventions that many of us remember because we lived through it. I'm talking about the Internet.

The Internet: Doomed To Spectacularly Collapse

In 1969, two computers at two different university campuses connected for the very first time. A simple message was broadcast, and the operators watched the screen with bated breath. The word was 'LOGIN'. But only the letters 'L' and 'O' arrived.

This had never been done before.

This demonstrated that data from one computer could be transmitted far and wide to another computer in a matter of seconds. While the initial test seemed like a failure at the time, it marked a profound turning point in the evolution of modern communication.

Now, like all new technologies, the Internet had its growing pains, especially when its competitors owned ink by the barrel, had printing presses as far as the eye could see and went by the names of the New York Times and the Wall Street Journal. These institutions had control over the public perception, which made them rich and incredibly powerful. And they saw the Internet as one thing only: a threat.

You see, these corporations had a monopoly on the way information was distributed to the public, but they also controlled the narrative. And when one 'official' channel has control of information, you could very well be exposed to one side of the story, while the other remains hidden. The Internet changed all that completely.

In the age of the Internet, information could be shared from anywhere. We were used to reading about big world events in the papers, but now we could also read directly from a blogger on the other side of the planet on a free open-source platform. The Internet gave us exposure to many points of view, rather than just one.

Not surprisingly, this upset the powers that be.

The Internet fought an uphill battle for years to get where it is today because its competitors, the most powerful media corporations in the world had, up until then, controlled the flow of information. These corporations could (and did) manipulate public opinion in accordance with a political or financial agenda.

By now, it will come as no surprise that they were slandering the Internet at the time.

> "The Internet is a FAD. Most things that succeed don't require retraining 250 million people."

> "I predict the Internet will soon go spectacularly supernova and in 1996 catastrophically collapse."

> "No online database will replace your daily newspaper, no CD-ROM can take the place of a competent teacher, and no computer network will change the way governments work."

I don't need to tell you how that worked out. The majority of the planet uses the Internet and we've never been more reliant on it.

Are you starting to see a similar pattern with new disruptive technologies? And does any of this sound familiar to the narratives around Bitcoin and cryptocurrencies today? This is why I liken this time to the pre-adoption period of any major advancement that has revolutionised our world.

It's a natural instinct to fear what we don't know, which is why disruptive technologies take time to be fully adopted. This in itself is a cycle which can be predictable and cause short-sightedness and fear. Anything that is a major leap in innovation, or disrupts the monopoly of big industries, will have an army of naysayers predicting its demise. Why? Because disruptive technologies have to first live in a world with the technology it's replacing, whether the infrastructure is there yet or not. Otherwise, it wouldn't be 'disruptive', right? There would be nothing to disrupt.

These technologies that drastically changed the way we live never experienced a linear growth pattern. They went through several major boom and bust cycles before gaining the amount of adoption they have today. Crypto is no different. It's simply in the middle of its cycle to mainstream adoption. Only this time, crypto is changing the way we send and receive wealth and disrupting a multi trillion-dollar industry that has been operating on nothing but a promise.

Our legacy financial system is now a runaway train that nobody can stop. It's no longer a matter of if, but when this train will derail, and more importantly, what will be there to replace it when it does? And if we had the opportunity to invest, would we capitalise on it?

Something to think about.

I Will Never Forget This Audience Member

In the summer of 2019 before the COVID lockdowns, my brother and I were hosting a live event with over 200 audience members. My brother was mid-presentation on stage when an audience member suddenly stood up, waved his hands around in frustration, stormed out of the room and slammed the doors loudly behind him. It was a very strange and dramatic moment. During the break, dozens of people gathered around to ask him what was wrong, and this is what he said:

"I've seen the DWG team present before, when Bitcoin was at an all-time low and everyone was saying it was a scam. I wanted to invest, but my friend talked me out of it, and I listened to him instead of doing my own research. I regret it now because I can see that I would be miles ahead if I hadn't listened to him. I'd be very likely retired."

This gentleman was angry at missing the opportunity when it presented itself. He followed popular opinion instead of being guided by market timing.

The Lesson

Be a contrarian and always do your own independent research.

Chapter 4

The Real Opportunity with Crypto

*Very few things on this planet open the doors to
immense levels of wealth.
Crypto is one of them.*

So now we've busted some of the myths and faced some of the fears around crypto, let's look at what crypto can do for you and your family. Everything I'm going to cover here has been experienced by myself and thousands of my students.

Life-Changing Gains of 10x, 100x, Even 10,000x

Crypto is considered to be one of those rare asset classes that have a host of asymmetric investment opportunities. Now, before your eyes glaze over and you dismiss this as financial jargon, stay with me because this information is crucial to unlocking the potential of this market.

An asymmetric opportunity means that for every $1 you invest, you have the potential to make $10 or more, while your risk remains capped at the initial $1. This is one of the reasons crypto is so appealing. There's an abundance of asymmetric opportunities and you don't need a five- or six-figure capital investment to make great gains. A modest investment of even $100 can possibly return $1,000 or more while your risk stays at the $100 you started with. Remember the $983 I invested into NEO that returned over $100,000 back in 2017? My risk was capped at the initial $983 investment I placed in the market.

This concept fundamentally changes the investment game because you now have the potential to unlock exponential gains without exposing yourself to excessive risk.

But here's where it gets interesting ... Crypto not only presents asymmetric investments, it's also been known to produce gains of anywhere from 1,000% to 80,000% and more. Whilst this level of gain isn't a guarantee, there are certain windows of opportunity that we can capitalise on if we invest smartly. And when we're talking about crypto, having some skin in the game is better than none.

Kate from Perth, Western Australia, Turns $4,000 into $85,600 in Two Months

In March 2020, DWG student Kate invested $4,000 into a cryptocurrency. Her investment went parabolic, and she turned that amount into a total of $85,600.

Now if you think that's impressive, had Kate just bought and held, she would have turned her $4,000 into $9,800,000 because that particular cryptocurrency rallied 244,900% from the date she sold.

> **The Lesson**
>
> Never remove your entire position at once.

An Early Retirement

When I tell people I was able to retire at thirty thanks to crypto investing, I'm met with a range of responses—everything from raised eyebrows to complete disbelief! But for me, this was a natural evolution once I learned what crypto can do and how to invest in it safely. By educating myself, I knew what was coming and could capitalise on opportunities every step of the way.

So, what was my secret?

It's about time: timing your entry into the market, and your time *in* the market. These are two separate yet connected concepts. By mastering them, I was able to put maximum upside potential in front of me—enough to be able to retire at such a young age. I took the time to learn about this asset, applied the concepts of market timing and human emotions, and continued to cultivate a mindset of abundance and self-sovereignty. And I invite you to do the same.

Is this about telling you that you can get rich overnight by investing in shiny crypto coins one, two and three? No, it's about something far more profound—giving you the tools to create wealth and freedom in all areas of your life, including your finances. I'll reveal the knowledge and methods that, when executed correctly, will put all the odds in your favour for an early retirement in as little as two to four years. If that sounds like too long to wait, let's put it into perspective by comparing it to our traditional retirement model:

Crypto model for retirement: Devote the time to educating yourself, investing safely and working with the market cycles of crypto and you can potentially secure a lifetime of financial freedom and an early retirement.

Traditional model for retirement: Work seven to eight hour days, five days per week, year in and year out, and you'll potentially be able to retire in thirty to fifty years.

I know which one I'd choose.

They say fortune favours the bold, but when it comes to crypto, it equally favours the patient.

An Equal Playing Field

When it comes to traditional financial markets such as stocks and bonds, the playing field is anything but level. Investors with deep knowledge and deeper pockets often dominate these markets, but crypto is entirely different. Why? Because it's a whole new ball game and in cryptocurrencies, everyone walks through the same door.

The wonderful thing about crypto is that it attracts people from all walks of life. It levels the playing field and gives everyone, irrespective of experience, the opportunity to participate in a ground-breaking financial revolution. You could devote one week to your crypto education and potentially know as much or even more about crypto than a traditional economist with decades of financial experience. There's no implied knowledge with crypto and this is one of the things that's so exciting and empowering about it. In traditional finance, you might need to go through a complex and costly educational process to invest in stocks or bonds, but with crypto, you can get yourself up to speed in a fraction of that time. Once you've grasped the lingo and understand the key concepts and safety rules, you can fast track your entry into this market. Just remember that every successful crypto investor once stood where you stand today. Every single one of us had the same learning curve.

"Spend each day trying to be a little wiser than you woke up."
Charlie Munger

Once upon a time the Internet seemed daunting and technical, now it's an integral and seamless part of our lives. I believe crypto will have a similar trajectory. So never let the crypto sector scare you off. We all walked through that same door, and we all can benefit from being early adopters and positioning ourselves well.

A Consistent Passive Income of $500-$1,500 Extra Per Week

So, if you buy at the right time, and wait for your coins to go up, is that as good as you can expect? No, in fact, we're just getting started. Believe it or not, there's another game-changing element that can skyrocket the performance of your portfolio, and many investors don't even know about it. It's called staking.

Staking operates in a similar way to traditional term deposits; except the interest you can earn with staking far outperforms anything you're used to earning today. It works like this: you agree to lock up a certain amount of your crypto for an agreed-upon duration (which varies from days to years) in exchange for a generous interest rate. And when I say generous, I'm talking about a much higher yield than you would receive from a traditional bank. With crypto, interest payouts of anywhere from 5% to as high as 1,000% APY (Annual Percentage Yield) are there for the taking.

It's no wonder crypto investors call it a license to print money.

But here's the cherry on top: while your crypto is staked and working for you, its value is pegged to the market. This means that the interest you are generating can potentially increase as the price of your crypto rises. So, you've now turned your asset into a productive asset that is generating you a (potentially very lucrative) passive income.

This is how some six-figure portfolios can crack seven figures in a bull market. They are earning yield on top of yield (more on this later). It's a double whammy of increased value and amplified interest—an upward spiral of wealth accumulation.

As you can see, digging a little deeper into the world of cryptocurrencies is well worth it, and this is just one of the many ways you can scale your portfolio and make it worth for you. I'll be diving into different scaling and passive income strategies later in this book.

The Same Opportunity as the Internet? The Internet 2.0

Imagine being transported back to the late eighties or early nineties and someone whispers in your ear about this revolutionary thing called the Internet. They say it will completely change the world, and there is a short window of time in which you can invest in it and be part of history. If you had the chance to get in at the ground level of such a game-changing new technology, would you do it? Because that's the opportunity we currently have with cryptocurrencies.

For anyone who remembers a time before the Internet, you'll know just how much of a paradigm shift it was. Colossal shifts in technology like this happen once, maybe twice in a lifetime. We've already witnessed the first. I believe crypto is the second.

The Internet brought us instant transmission of data, crypto brings us instant transmission of value.

I have no doubt we are witnessing the completion of the Internet, the missing piece of the puzzle that will prompt innovation in all corners of the globe. Just as the Internet reshaped the way we communicate, share information and connect globally, cryptocurrency is poised to completely overhaul our financial world, and it's already well on its way.

So, consider this your invitation—not solely as an investment opportunity, but as a chance to be part of history. The finance sector will not only be democratised, it will be completely rebuilt.

Freedom to Live Life on Your Terms

One of the cornerstones of cryptocurrencies is the idea of financial freedom, so let's look at the other ways crypto opens the door to freedom in our lives:

> **Freedom to choose.** Having decentralised options for investing and storing money means we no longer need to have it locked up in a legacy banking system that doesn't serve us. We can have our funds in our control at all times, to move around as we see fit.
>
> **Freedom to feel sovereign.** Education takes time, but it's an investment that will pay dividends in the future. Learning about alternatives to traditional finance gives us options to step out of old patterns and into true self-sovereignty for perhaps the first time in our lives.
>
> **Financial Freedom.** The ability to completely pay off a mortgage, help family members or friends, and never have to worry about where money is coming from again.

Freedom to have a plan B. When the rules can change at any given moment, it becomes more important than ever to have a plan B.

Freedom for debt and loans. Complete financial freedom means not having to rely on any person or institution for assistance ever again.

Yes, I truly believe crypto can give you all of this and so much more. I've seen it and experienced it many times. And what I see from my clients is that once they've achieved their initial goals for crypto, different priorities start to emerge and it can be things they've never thought of before. This is wonderful because when you reach a point of seeing potential and freedom that can be yours, you truly stop restricting yourself and start to see that *anything* is possible.

Seeing the Big Picture

All these opportunities are available to anyone who is willing to put the time and effort into learning about this asset class. There are many gifts to be uncovered, and many layers of opportunity within this world. In fact, what we discuss here is really just the tip of the iceberg when it comes to the opportunity in cryptocurrencies.

Many people believe this space is all about Bitcoin and Ethereum, but there are hundreds of cryptocurrencies that can generate additional income and give you so much more. That's why educating yourself, staying out of fear, and ignoring the crypto naysayers is the best way to start this journey.

So many people around the world have had success with cryptocurrencies. Their stories alone should ignite a spark of curiosity about this new financial world. The journey to ultimate wealth begins with the desire to learn what this incredible asset class is all about.

Chapter 5

Bullish Catalysts That Will Drive Market Prices

Knowing what's coming and positioning ourselves accordingly is the single biggest advantage we have when it comes to investing in crypto.

At this point, you may be asking, 'How are these gains even possible?' Well, it all comes down to market drivers, or what I like to refer to as 'bullish catalysts'.

Bullish catalysts are the real-world factors that drive value into this market. With each cycle, this value doesn't just increase, it becomes an immeasurable force, influenced by large-scale adoption on both a retail and institutional level.

We've seen it once before in 2017 when crypto first hit centre stage for retail adoption. The Ethereum blockchain had been launched, and it paved the way for a number of aspiring cryptocurrencies to crowdfund their visions and bring investment and innovation into the space. This included an explosion of new coins and projects in the form of ICOs (Initial Coin Offerings) bringing millions of new users and a tonne of value into the space.

Another catalyst was the institutional FOMO of 2023 and beyond, when traditional finance began lodging applications to provide crypto-related financial services through Bitcoin Spot ETFs (Exchange Traded Funds).

Will there be more events that drive people to crypto going forward? Absolutely, and I'm going to share them in this chapter. These are clear catalysts that will redefine the narrative around crypto and propel this market to new heights with each consecutive cycle. You can use these as part of your investment approach because when you know what's coming, who is coming and when they are coming, you can position yourself accordingly.

In crypto, there's a term called 'diamond hands', which refers to an investor's ability to hold strong and steady through any market shakeups. And trust me, the market has gone through cataclysmic shake ups with plenty more to come! That's why this information is so important. Look at it as a solid foundation of opportunity, strengthening your diamond hands and giving you the power to hold through the downturns and overcome the market volatility.

So, with that said, let's dive into my top four bullish catalysts.

Bullish Catalyst 1: The Economy Skating on Thin Ice

Let's start with the elephant in the room: our financial system is dancing on a tightrope of uncertainty. Look around and you'll see huge cracks in the foundation, from global uncertainty to the cost-of-living crisis and the squeeze on small businesses that can no longer survive. We've seen banks and financial institutions trembling on the brink of collapse, while others were taken over by regulators. We've witnessed plummeting stocks, threats of bank runs, political unrest and a whole lot of fear and distrust.

And then there's the debt.

If we take a look at the US, which currently is the largest economy in the world, we'll see that debt has been ballooning to unprecedented levels for years. In fact, it's hard to find a historical parallel.

How bad is it? Well, in the USA alone, in the ninety-five years between 1913 and 2008, $8.8 trillion worth of debt was created and since 2008, more than $22 trillion has been added. This alone should send shivers up anyone's spine. In my opinion, it's a runaway train and there's nothing but a cataclysmic event that will stop it.

Why should we care about this debt? Because debt creates inflation, and inflation is a hidden tax on your savings.

The more debt a country accumulates, the more money is printed and the more it floods the economy so that interest rates soar, and the prices of groceries and everyday items spiral out of control. Suddenly, your hard-earned savings are dwindling in value and if your money isn't keeping up with inflation, you're paying the hidden tax on your savings that many aren't aware of.

In Australia, we can see that inflation went from 1.1% in early 2021, to almost 8% in 2023, all while wages stayed the same and interest rates aggressively climbed.[1] It's clear for everyone to see that we're getting much less for our dollar and this 'shrinkflation' is becoming a major problem.

How does anyone survive in this modern world?

Billionaire Cameron Winklevoss sums it up perfectly:

"Imagine paying a money manager 7.9% a year to do absolutely nothing with your money. That's what inflation is. It's a hidden management fee that comes with no return. Today, if you hold USD cash, you are paying the US government 7.9% to do nothing with your money. Scary."

And how are governments responding to this crisis? Well, they are printing money, handing out stimulus packages, announcing inflation targets and promising to bail out struggling institutions. Make no mistake, this is a double-edged sword that is eroding the value of our currency and steering us toward an inevitable economic catastrophe.

What. A. Mess!

When governments do too much inflating, we end up with a situation like Venezuela, where a severe economic crisis has devalued the national currency so much it's become nearly worthless. In fact, cash is being used to create art sculptures to sell to tourists, because it's worth more that way.

This is not just alarming, it's completely unsustainable.

So why is all of this bullish for crypto? Quite simply because crypto gives us a ticket out of this global mess. It's considered a flight to safety—despite its volatility.

You see, the legacy banking system has struggled with the same problems for decades while in the relatively short time Bitcoin has been around, it's only increased in value, utility and support—all without aggressive hyperinflation. The fragility of our legacy system has been exposed, and people no longer want to bear the brunt of something so broken.

It's time for a plan B!

Many ordinary people are fed up with the current regime and they're looking for an exit strategy. They're sick of the big banks, sick of centralised control and no longer want to be at the mercy of these institutions and their destructive methods. I believe we're witnessing the final death throes of a beast that has ruled for far too long and we'll see many more financial institutions collapse in the coming years. We need to be preparing our financial life raft so we can chart a course out of this global mess.

And where are some of the savviest minds in the financial world heading? They're turning to crypto.

Many of the smartest economists, hedge fund managers and well-known financial figures are throwing their weight behind cryptocurrencies. They've begun to recognise it as a pivotal part of our economic future. We're about to see millions of new users enter the crypto market as a flight to financial security and more stability.

It's not a matter of if, but when.

Bullish Catalyst 2: The Greatest Wealth Transfer in History Is About to Happen

The second bullish catalyst is when millennials overtake baby boomers as the world's largest living adult generation and the dominant working and investing force. Investors are calling this the greatest wealth transfer of our time.

Now, millennials can have a bad reputation. We've all heard the narrative that they're lazy, they don't want to work and they're obsessed with technology. We've also seen the headlines stating millennials will retire poorer and own less property than any previous generations, despite being more educated. The overarching theme appears to be that millennials don't stand much of a chance financially.

But here's what people are forgetting. Millennials have overtaken baby boomers as America's largest generation. In 2022, they numbered 72.24 million, compared to Gen X at approximately 65.37 million and baby boomers at 68.59 million.[2] And when they are predicted to hit peak domination in 2028, there will be 95.8 million millennials in the US alone. Their influence will have an undeniable impact on the world's biggest economies and industries. A wave of capital is about to be transferred to millennials and it will absolutely change our world.

In the USA alone, baby boomers will hand down $68 trillion in one of the greatest wealth transfers in human history.

So, what are millennials investing in? If all this money is about to come into their hands, where do we think it will go?

We only need to look at the data.

The Charles Schwab Report from Q3 2019 shows that the fifth largest investment category for millennials' self-directed 401k is the Grayscale Bitcoin Trust.[3] This demonstrates that millennials are already investing in Bitcoin while Gen X and baby boomers had no rankings for crypto in their top ten.

A CNBC survey revealed that 83% of millennial millionaires own cryptocurrencies, in stark contrast to older generations of millionaires.[4] More than half of these millennial millionaires have at least 50% of their wealth in crypto, and nearly a third have at least three-quarters of their wealth in crypto.

Let's just pause here for a moment. What these astonishing statistics show us is exactly where millennials see value. It's very clear they see it in crypto. It doesn't take a rocket scientist to understand what will happen with the biggest transfer of wealth when millennials overtake baby boomers as the largest living generation. Not to mention the generations to follow, including Gen Z and Generation Alpha.

Now let's compare this to how millennials see gold.

In 2020, Morgan Stanley's Chief Global Strategist and Head of Emerging Markets publicly affirmed that millennial investors prefer Bitcoin over holding gold. They see gold as stagnant, antiquated and disconnected from their social and shareable lifestyles. Crypto, on the other hand, has a fun, social and shareable element to it, particularly non-fungible tokens (NFTs) which have transformed the way digital assets are perceived and shared. They're not just pieces of code. They represent artwork, collectibles and unique digital gifts that hold value in the virtual world. It's very easy to gift an NFT to a friend, family member or favourite influencer. This adds a whole new dimension to the investment experience and creates an engaging way for millennials to express themselves.

This is in stark contrast to holding a block of gold locked up in a safe.

And look at what's already happening with payment providers. Some of the biggest in the industry have opened the door to crypto payments by linking their cards to crypto. According to a 2022 survey conducted by Deloitte, 75% of retailers have plans to start accepting cryptocurrencies over the next two years.[5]

In fact, in 2021, the Bitcoin network overtook PayPal for transaction volume for the quarter with the Bitcoin network processing an estimated average of $489 billion per quarter, compared to PayPal's average of $302 billion per quarter.[6] Whilst it has a long way to go to overtake the world's leading payment providers such as Visa and Mastercard, it is well on its way.

Remember, millennials are the first generation to grow up with widespread access to the Internet and digital technology. They're rewriting the traditional playbook when it comes to generating income. Rather than following conventional career paths, this generation is drawn to online ventures, entrepreneurship and a lifestyle that is supported by a digital presence in some way or another.

And what about the generation after millennials, the true digital natives, Gen Z? How do you think their preferences are going to shape advancements and innovations in digital sectors? These are the generations who have grown up watching their parents struggle in a system that doesn't work.

Here are some interesting statistics from an official survey conducted by Facebook[7] in 2016:

- 45% of millennials are open to switching banks, credit cards and brokerage accounts
- 44% do not feel their bank understands them
- Only 8% trust financial institutions

This means 92% of millennials do not trust banks.

So, they don't trust banks, they're known as the digital generation and they're looking for another option. What do you think they will turn to? As they become the dominant generation with money, will they want to keep supporting the legacy system that has proven itself to fail?

Somehow, I don't think so.

We have to remember that each generation perceives value differently. If we rewind the clock back to the 1970s and 1980s, baby boomers were at the helm of innovation. That era brought us personal computers and the rise of tech giants like Apple and Microsoft, but it was met with scepticism and misunderstanding by the generation that came before. To them, these devices seemed like peculiar gadgets or irrelevant novelties. Little did they realize they were witnessing something that would redefine the way we live, work and play.

For Generation X, the disruptive tech of the time was email, text messaging, Google and Amazon. Once again, the generation before was perplexed. These technologies seemed so impersonal, and contrary to the way they socialised at the time. But just look at the impact these technologies have had on our world.

Which brings us to today, and the digital revolution taking place:

Currently, we have:

- The world's most popular media company, Facebook, which creates no content
- The world's largest taxi firm, Uber, which owns no cars
- The world's largest accommodation provider, Airbnb, which owns no property

What comes next?

A global currency, cryptocurrency, which has no bank.

So, even though it can be overwhelming, we have to remember that innovation will speed ahead, whether we are onboard or not. And new technology will always exist in a world that doesn't understand it first.

In other words, *you don't have to resonate with the direction to benefit from the investment opportunity.*

In summary, millennials are about to become the predominant generation with money. We know they are drawn to all things digital. We know they prefer Bitcoin over gold. We know that many of the millionaires in their generation have made their money through crypto.

Something to think about.

Bullish Catalyst 3: Wall Street's Greed

So, we've heard about the economic outlook and the biggest generation who will be shaping our future for years to come. Now let's talk about the powerhouse that will drive the crypto market to a multitrillion-dollar asset class and beyond: Wall Street.

In 2023, the estimated number of global crypto users passed 420 million. That's 4.2% of the population holding some form of cryptocurrency.[8] What's fascinating is that this demographic largely consists of retail investors, with very early institutional involvement only.

What does this mean and why is it so bullish?

Allow me to explain.

For a long time, major institutions/traditional finance have been unable to offer crypto services due to regulatory red tape, namely from the SEC (Securities Exchange Commission) in the US. Everything from asset classification and custody issues, to accounting and taxation processes has gone through the scrutinizing and outdated eye of these regulatory bodies. It's been a long process that has slowed their entry into crypto, and I can understand why.

These institutions are responsible for enormous amounts of money for millions of users worldwide. They can't entrust a start-up crypto exchange with billions and trillions of dollars. Where would these assets be stored? And who would hold the private keys?

Put simply, entering crypto posed substantial challenges for these institutions. You could say that the infrastructure just wasn't there. So, just like the automobile, electricity and the Internet, the infrastructure had to be developed in order for the full potential of the technology to be available and recognised.

For years we've been saying that institutions will drive one of the largest crypto-fuelled rallies to come and the green light from these regulatory bodies will bring a tidal wave of capital into this market over many months and years. It's never been a case of 'if' it will happen. It's always been a case of 'when'.

In 2023, the race kicked off and institution after institution began lodging Bitcoin Spot ETF (Exchange Traded Fund) applications to the SEC which were then approved in January of 2024. These are essentially products that allow everyday investors to buy Bitcoin through an institution, without having to actually own and manage it themselves. It's privatised, centralised crypto 'ownership', meaning you don't hold the private keys, the financial institution does. For many investors this is an appealing offer, despite the fact that this goes against the core principles of self-custody that cryptocurrency was created for.

For decades, Wall Street has been synonymous with power, influence and greed, and the rise of cryptocurrencies presents a paradigm shift they can't afford to ignore. If they can't beat us, they will find a way to join us. I'm reminded of a popular quote that has been attributed to Ghandi:

> "First they ignore you, then they laugh at you, then they fight you, then you win."

Wall Street has recognised there is a major gap in the market to fill. The bottleneck has been released, and the wave of institutional investment has begun to build, bringing awareness and adoption with it in a monumental way. Make no mistake, institutional FOMO and Wall Street's greed will be the engine that powers global adoption over the next decade. This is a wave that will never, ever slow down. It will continue to build and grow, and I believe there's no turning back.

And what are the savvy investors doing? They are quietly adding to their portfolio using market timing and front running this institutionally fuelled rally as best as they can.

Traditional finance entering crypto comes with a silver lining. It brings more credibility to the space, along with wide scale adoption and capital, but at the cost of privacy, more centralisation and yes—more control. But that's only the case if you decide to hand it over. There will always be self-custody options in crypto, and there will always be decentralisation. As long as you have a wallet that you control, where *you* own the private keys, your crypto assets are safe.

Which brings us to the other important factor driving this bullish catalyst. The supply shock.

You see, Bitcoin Spot ETFs require a 1:1 backing. This means for every Bitcoin an investor purchases through their services, they need to hold the actual Bitcoin in their holdings.

Which begs the question. *Where will all these Bitcoins come from?*

A surge in the demand for Bitcoin will create a major supply shock, powered by an increase in retail adoption and the halving event (which I discuss next).

The crypto market will undergo unprecedented growth as the bridge between traditional finance and digital assets becomes stronger. It's a place where money meets innovation, and we have a front-row seat.

Bullish Catalyst 4: Every Four Years … This Happens

We've talked about the problems in our fiat currency system, with governments around the world printing money, devaluing currencies and leaving the door wide open for hyperinflation. Well, traditional companies are guilty of this too. At any time, they can dilute the value of their existing shares by simply issuing more stock.

Bitcoin, however, is wired differently. It's pre-programmed to have a maximum supply of 21 million Bitcoin—period. Bitcoin can't be 'printed' into existence whenever it suits a central authority. Its maximum supply is fixed. This number cannot and will not be changed ever. Let's look at this a little closer.

Rather than being printed by banks, Bitcoin is 'mined', which is the process of digitally 'extracting' new Bitcoins by solving complex mathematical problems. The mining process ensures the security, integrity, and decentralised nature of the Bitcoin network. When a mining pool cracks the complex code, miners are rewarded with a certain amount of Bitcoin every ten minutes. This process can be compared to gold mining in several ways.

To start, just as gold mining is the process of extracting precious metal from the ground, Bitcoin mining is the process of obtaining new Bitcoins from the digital world. Gold miners use tools and equipment to extract gold from the Earth. Bitcoin miners use powerful computers to validate and record transactions on the Bitcoin network. Gold miners are rewarded with gold. Bitcoin miners are rewarded with Bitcoin.

Gold mining becomes more difficult as the gold gets depleted. It's not as easy to access and requires more expensive equipment to mine. Bitcoin mining becomes more challenging as more miners participate in the network, and it requires more computing power. At the start, gold was plentiful, and picks and shovels were more than enough to find it, however as global retail adoption took place, those picks and shovels were no longer enough. Bigger, faster and more expensive mining equipment such as cranes and pulleys were required to achieve the same result. A similar thing has happened with Bitcoin.

If we rewind the clock back to 2009, developers and programmers who were mining for Bitcoin didn't need the computing power they need today. Back then, a couple of computers running at home could produce fifty Bitcoin every ten minutes. This is how Bitcoin billionaires were made. It was incredibly profitable for those who held for the long term to say the least.

So why should you care about this? Because halving events *will* affect supply. You see, every four years, the Bitcoin computer program and algorithms become increasingly harder to crack. As a result, the amount of Bitcoin coming into circulating supply gets cut in half.

Yes, you read right, *the supply of new Bitcoin entering the market gets cut in half.*

It looks a little like this:
2008 – 50 Bitcoin rewarded every ten minutes
2012 – 25 Bitcoin rewarded every ten minutes
2016 – 12.5 Bitcoin rewarded every ten minutes
2020 – 6.25 Bitcoin rewarded every ten minutes
2024 – 3.125 Bitcoin rewarded every ten minutes
2028 – 1.56 Bitcoin rewarded every ten minutes
2032 – 0.78 Bitcoin rewarded every ten minutes

These halving events are programmed into the code. They will happen, and they'll continue to happen until 2140 when the last Bitcoin is mined.

To gain some perspective on this, miners who held their mined Bitcoin from 2009 would have technically been generating:

$1,000,000 every ten minutes, if today's price was $20,000 per Bitcoin.

$2,500,000 every ten minutes, if today's price was $50,000 per Bitcoin.

$5,000,000 every ten minutes, if today's price was $100,000 per Bitcoin.

As you can see, early adopters of Bitcoin who understood its true value were able to create enough wealth for generations to come and beyond! This is one example of how playing the long game in crypto can reward you.

So, why is this important for timing your entry into the market? Well, it's about supply and demand.

Consider this: if we all found out that in three months' time, the rate at which gold comes out of the ground would be cut in half, what do you think would happen to the price? Would investor numbers increase if everyone knew the supply of gold was about to drastically reduce?

I think we all know the answer.

This is what's known as a supply shock, and it happens to Bitcoin every four years, thanks to the halving events. Understanding this is another key to your success in this market because we all know that a diminishing supply results in a surging demand. If this is guaranteed to occur every four years, we can and should use it to our advantage.

If we examine the previous halving events that have taken place since Bitcoin's inception, we'll notice two things:

1. The market grows exponentially in the months leading up to the halving.
2. In the months following it, Bitcoin reaches all-time highs, and the bull market moves into full swing.

You can see the positive price action after the Bitcoin halving event has taken place place (dashed line between II and III) in the following chart:

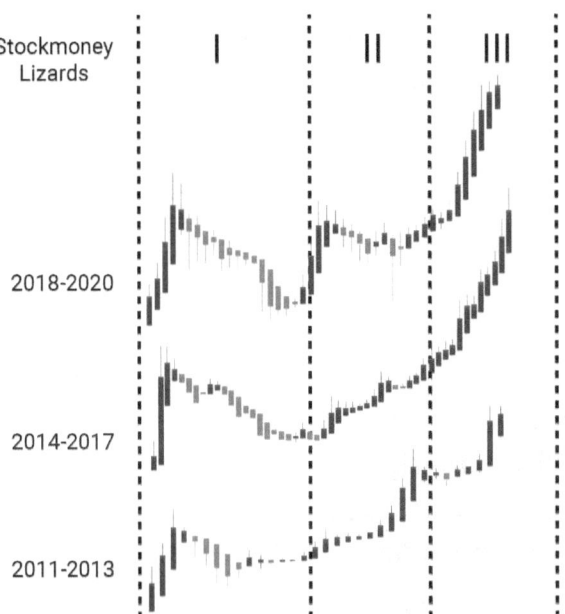

Are you starting to see the big picture?

You may be surprised to learn that it's not just the halving event that reduces the supply of Bitcoin. It's also investor negligence.

Reports have estimated that as of September 2023, approximately 6 million Bitcoin have been lost forever.[9] That's approximately 30% of the supply. This is mainly due to new investors making costly mistakes and not protecting their private keys. That number is astonishing, not only from a security perspective but also from a supply perspective. It means that up to 6 million Bitcoin will never be sold and placed back into the market. They are out of the market's hands—forever.

And do I think that number of lost Bitcoin will continue to climb? Absolutely.

So, not only do we have the Bitcoin halving reducing the new supply by half, but we also have the continued misplacement of Bitcoin that will forever be removed from the circulating supply. Bitcoin will be met with constant supply shocks as the demand for it increases.

And if you think that's bullish, let's discuss the scarcity of Bitcoin.

As of April 2024, Bitcoin is the most scarce asset on the planet due to the time it takes to replenish the current supply. In 2023, gold was considered to be the most scarce asset because each year only 3,000 tonnes of gold is mined. The current gold stock globally was 185,000 tonnes, so it would take approximately sixty-two years to replenish all the gold on the planet. Compare this with Bitcoin which, after the April 2024 halving event, would take 121 years to replenish the current stock.

This is why Bitcoin will become the most scarce asset on the planet. In fact some investors believe that individuals who hold an entire Bitcoin will one day be given a special name due to the rarity and cost per coin.

Are these bullish catalysts the closest thing to knowing the future?

In my opinion, yes. This is the beauty of knowing what's coming and positioning ourselves accordingly.

To Summarise

Many investors outside this market have no idea these seismic shifts are underway. They're unaware of the huge changes these will bring with them, but you *are now informed*.

- Wall Street's greed will power global adoption, whether we like it or not
- Bitcoins circulating supply will be cut in half every four years, whether we like it or not
- Millennials will drive trillions of dollars of investment value in this market, whether we like it or not

And global macroeconomic uncertainty will drive millions of new users and trillions of capital into this market as investors search for financial security and a plan B.

It's not a matter of if, but when.

Arming yourself with this knowledge and using these catalysts to your advantage will place you miles ahead of the game. And when you time your market entry (as we discuss next), you'll be aligning yourself to a potential early retirement like many of my students have before. The wave of wealth is coming. It's going to be like nothing else we've seen so far.

Are you ready?

Chapter 6

When Opportunity Knocks, Will You Answer?

If it's too easy, it's too late.

The above phrase reminds us that the most significant gains come to those who are early adopters.

For many years, crypto was the realm of the developer and the sovereign minded. Those of us who intentionally sought to distance ourselves from traditional banks and financial middlemen. We put in the time and effort to learn about this asset class, and let me tell you, it wasn't always easy. We navigated new applications, unfamiliar tools and many platforms that were in their infancy. And just like today, there was no Bank of Bitcoin to contact if you made a mistake. There have been many barriers to entry over the years, but those who saw crypto's potential, studied the cycles and invested with the patterns have reaped the financial rewards.

So, what does this mean for you?

Well, the incredible gains and market cycles we've witnessed so far have mostly come from early retail investors. Can you imagine what will happen when the titans of big finance enter the scene? While crypto was never invented for them, their involvement will expose cryptocurrencies to hundreds of millions of new investors, including the super and retirement fund market. This signals crypto's inevitable shift from the fringes of the financial world when it was first created to the mainstream. As crypto technologies mature and adoption increases, the early bird advantage steadily dwindles.

So, I ask you: *Will you jump at this once in a lifetime opportunity?*

In my view, the crypto market is at a pivotal juncture. Millions of new users are preparing to enter over the next few years and the demand will soar. Can you imagine the impact global adoption will have on cryptocurrency values? As institutional investors join the charge, it will propel crypto prices to all new heights!

The opportunity of a lifetime awaits, but it won't wait forever. To truly harness the transformative potential of crypto, we must be ready to jump when opportunity knocks.

The crypto market waits for no one.

Let's Hear from Our Students

Justine, 78 and Terry, 81
Gold Coast, Queensland, Australia

"Since venturing into the world of cryptocurrency, our investments have experienced remarkable growth. Starting with an initial $100,000 AUD investment in major projects, along with $500 in each of twenty-one other coins, our portfolio has now grown to $980,432 AUD. Additionally, we ventured into another project, which now has a staked value of $2,690,000 USD today.

These astounding figures can be attributed to the guidance of our expert coaches.

Beyond the financial gains, our cryptocurrency journey has allowed us to achieve significant life goals. It has provided a reassuring supplement to our superannuation, which was yielding diminishing returns. More importantly, it has enabled us to financially support our children and grandchildren, bringing immense joy to our lives."

**Rob and Caroline,
Perth, Western Australia**

"In our journey through the world of cryptocurrency, we've achieved remarkable success. With an initial investment of just over $8,000, we've seen our portfolio grow to an impressive $400,000 in approximately sixteen months.

But the impact of this journey goes beyond numbers. We've been able to achieve life-changing milestones that were once distant dreams. Thanks to our crypto investments, we now have the means to pay off our home mortgage, a goal we never thought possible without winning the lottery.

This journey has not only transformed our financial future, but has also opened our eyes to the incredible potential of cryptocurrency. It's a powerful tool for reshaping lives and achieving newfound financial freedom."

PART TWO

Key Crypto Investing Secrets

Welcome to Part 2 of this incredible crypto investing journey!

So far, we've covered why cryptocurrencies were invented, the fears new investors may have, the real value this technology brings and the bullish catalysts that will drive crypto into a multitrillion-dollar asset class. By now you're probably wondering how to get started?

Great question.

Before we dive into the step-by-step instructions, it's important to have a basic understanding of how this market actually works—specifically the importance of fundamental analysis and human emotions. Why? Because it could mean the difference between potentially retiring early or mis-timing the market and giving up on crypto altogether. Huge, to say the least.

Could you skip this section, jump to Part 3 and go straight into buying different cryptos? Yes, but that would be like setting off on a road trip without a map—there's a high chance you could get lost, you'll probably take a few wrong turns, and you could end up somewhere completely different to where you wanted to go. I can say from years of experience that understanding market cycles (fundamental analysis) and human emotions will play more of a role in your crypto success than the coins you hold. Markets are driven by these factors, and as long-term investors in this space, these are your keys to success.

I've taken the most crucial pieces of information and broken them down into easy-to-follow sections. These include:

- The difference between a bull market and a bear market
- Understanding human emotions and sentiment
- The key indicator in crypto and why you must follow it
- Mastering market cycles and timing your entry like a pro
- Inside a bull market and what to expect

You'll notice a large focus on Bitcoin throughout this section, without much mention of other cryptocurrencies. This is because Bitcoin is known as the reserve cryptocurrency, and what happens to Bitcoin tends to happen to the broader market. Understanding how Bitcoin behaves gives us valuable knowledge we can apply market wide.

In Part 3, we explore other cryptocurrencies, including growth sectors to focus on and how to diversify your portfolio. For now, let's learn about how the market actually works, so you can time your entry like a pro and begin building the portfolio of your dreams.

Let's dive in.

Key Terms & Translations

In this section we talk about:

Market: The entire crypto market and what it does.
Bear Market: Prices in a prolonged downward trajectory.
Bull Market: Prices in a prolonged upward trajectory.
Super Cycle: An entire cycle comprising a bull and bear market.
Market Sentiment: How the world *feels* towards crypto.
Contrarian: Acting in opposition to popular opinion.
Pull Back / Retracement / Correction: A drop in the price, often suddenly.
Recovery: Prices coming back after dropping, typically in a short timeframe.
Pump/Pumping: Prices going up quite aggressively in a short timeframe.
Capitulate/Bottoming Event: A cataclysmic event that drops the market suddenly, often indicating the bottom of a bear market and the all-time low for that cycle.

Chapter 7

The Difference Between a Bull Market and a Bear Market

"Accumulation in the bear market is as crucial as taking profits in the bull market."

Coach Alex, Digital Wealth Group

For anyone new to the investing world, there are two terms you'll hear over and over again. They are 'bull market' and 'bear market'. So, what's the difference between the two?

Bull = prices rising upward.

Bear = prices falling downward.

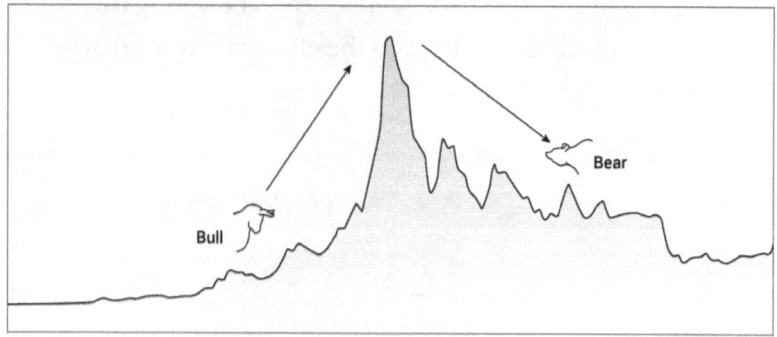

Bull Market

Picture a bull charging ahead, an unstoppable force with horns pointing to the sky. This signals a time of excitement in the crypto world when things are looking up and prices are on the rise.

Historically, the bull market kicks off some months (even years) after a bottoming event has taken place. A bottoming event is a time when the market has capitulated, and the outlook is quite negative. But as prices recover and start to rise for prolonged periods, confidence slowly returns. This positive price movement is indicative of the early bull market phase. It's not uncommon to have a series of short-term corrections on the way up to the next all-time high and pullbacks of 10-30% can be expected along the way, particularly with Bitcoin. These dips present excellent buying opportunities for investors wanting to enter during this time.

The other telltale sign of a bull market is the enthusiastic coverage in the media. Positive sentiment and contagious optimism spread far and wide as millions of retail investors, institutions and developers enter the space. This period of bullish sentiment tends to bring a surge of energy into the crypto market and we're likely to see increases in innovation, development and infrastructure during this time.

Bear Market

On the flip side, the bear market is denoted by the bear swiping its claws down—prices are falling, and the sentiment is usually more cautious and pessimistic. Historically, the bear market begins after the top has been identified and markets pull back. We enter a period of prolonged downward movement that can last for months or even years.

During a bear market, there's a noticeable decline in innovation, subdued sentiment and media coverage, and a slower pace of adoption. The allure of the market dwindles due to poor price performance, leading to diminished enthusiasm and an overall sense of wariness among investors.

As you can see, the bull and bear markets are like the ebb and flow of the financial world. We have optimism and positive movement on one side, and caution and subdued enthusiasm on the other.

So why is this so important to know? Because we want to time our entry so we buy in a bear market and sell in a bull market. In other words, 'buy the lows, sell the highs!'

As we move through Part 2, you'll learn to identify *exactly* where you are at any point in these cycles. This is key to timing the market well and placing maximum upside potential in front of you.

But first, I want to share a crucial concept when it comes to creating long-term wealth.

Chapter 8

Delay Gratification, Create Financial Freedom

Fortune favours the bold,
but also the patient when it comes to crypto.

Do you know what's rampant in the crypto world? Those 'get rich quick' schemes that sparkle like diamonds but disappear into dust. While a few investors might strike it lucky with these high-risk plays, they're like the unicorns of the crypto world—the exception, not the rule. That's why I advocate for a blueprint that is safe—long-term investment in foundational assets, plus strategic diversification in growth sectors. We want to build wealth from smart crypto investing, not just through sheer luck!

We should aim to have a section of our portfolio set up as low maintenance. This becomes our foundational portfolio, which is our stable, long-term play. It's almost like a 'set and forget' portion of our portfolio, where the market does the heavy lifting for us. From there, we can look to expand through growth sectors, passive income opportunities and more speculative assets that have the power to supercharge our portfolio to parabolic levels.

Delaying gratification is a crucial concept in the world of cryptocurrencies and is a healthy attitude to develop that will serve you time and time again. Wealth-building and stress-free gains can be made by simply resisting the temptation for immediate rewards and selling prematurely. When you know you're in it for the long term, you're not as susceptible to scammers who will prey on the desire for quick profits. Holding through market turbulence is a key principle I teach, and it leads to a more peaceful and confident investment journey.

Now let's move onto another key component of safe, strategic investing.

Chapter 9

Balance Your Emotions, Increase Your Gains

In the world of crypto investing, emotions play more of a role than you think.

When investors first enter the crypto space, they typically do so in a rush of excitement and euphoria. After all, this is a lucrative asset class that promises extraordinary returns. But that euphoria leads many to dive in headfirst, without knowing anything about market cycles or managing their emotions. And when it comes to crypto, these things play a crucial role.

In the years I've been involved in crypto, I've seen what can happen when people enter guns ablazing—impulsive decisions, improper research and following the sentiment of the crowd. And what is sentiment linked to? You guessed it: human emotions.

When the market is hot, people can become so gripped with greed that they buy their crypto when prices are sky high. They place maximum downside potential in front of them instead of upside. In other words, they don't give themselves much room to grow.

On the flip side, market downturns and bear cycles can evoke such fear among investors that they start panic-selling their crypto and fleeing the market in a frenzy. Rational judgment gets thrown out the window and they sell at a loss, at the worst possible time in the market cycle. Emotionally driven decisions like this can have significant consequences, so learning to tame them is key. While fear and greed are some of our most heightened states, neither of them creates a savvy investor.

I love a Warren Buffett quote that approaches things a little differently.

> "Be greedy when others are fearful. And fearful when others are greedy."

When the market is down, the sentiment and collective opinion around crypto is down, too. Many people are reluctant to invest at this time, but savvy investors are rubbing their hands together and buying up a storm. It feels counter-intuitive, but this is how many millionaires have been made.

So, what do these investors know that the average new investor doesn't? It all comes down to market psychology and human emotions. In the next chapter, I'll introduce you to some of the ways you can recognise and navigate global market sentiment.

Wealth Transfers from the Impatient to the Patient – Like It Did With Susan

In late 2019 during a live crypto presentation in front of 500 audience members in Sydney I met Susan, an entrepreneur who was enthusiastic about entering the crypto market. We were educating people about the next major market cycle about to unfold and why getting positions now would pay off in the next few years (possibly months). Susan was inspired to join the DWG program and get extra help.

Susan invested $200,000 USD into Bitcoin, which was hovering between $7,000-9,000 USD at the time. She accumulated over time at an average price of around $8,000 USD (which gave her around twenty-five Bitcoin). Susan was positioned well and set to ride the next major wave, but she was triggered into panic selling before she even got there. And she didn't just sell a few Bitcoin, she sold her *entire* position!

What caused Susan to react in such a fearful way and sell everything?
It was a short-term pullback, something that happens in the crypto market all the time.

You see, every journey to the bull market top is met with 10-30% pullbacks in price before re-correcting and moving upward once again. This is a fact of crypto markets, but it became too much pressure for Susan. When Bitcoin retraced to $5,000 USD momentarily, she sold her entire position and exited the market. Nothing we said convinced her to stop this emotional selling decision.

If Susan had bought and held, like we teach all our students, she would have seen Bitcoin rise to as high as $65,000 USD per coin in just over a year. Her portfolio would have reached $1.6 million USD in value.

The Lesson

Human emotions will have you running blind in this market if you don't understand their role and plan accordingly. Education and logic should always come before emotions in crypto investing. Always.

Chapter 10

Industry Tools to Navigate Crypto Markets

My single greatest piece of advice to any new investor is simple: Be a contrarian.

Now let's learn more about how to manage our emotions in crypto so they don't completely work against us. I can tell you that as predictable as market cycles are, they can also be brutal, and the emotional journey new investors go on is very real. So, I'm going to share two tools that will help you gauge not only your own emotions, but also the sentiment of the crowd.

1. The Wall Street Cheat Sheet

In financial markets, the 'Wall Street Cheat Sheet' documents the ups and downs of the investment cycle and the emotional highs and lows that investors tend to go through. It's a handy way to help you recognise and navigate the various stages of market sentiment.

The Wall Street Cheat Sheet isn't just crypto market related, it's *every* market related.

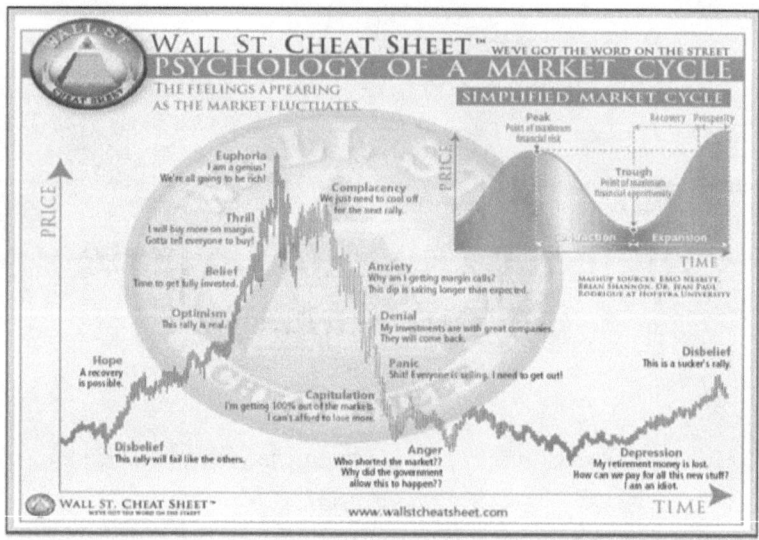

If you look at the chart, you'll see that as we approach the top of the super cycle (the peak), we enter a period of euphoria. This is when prices are at all-time highs and new investors are led to believe they're never coming down (a narrative often perpetuated by the media). In the euphoria stage, everyone is talking about crypto, and everyone is a fan. But here's the thing: this period is considered to be a time of maximum financial risk.

Conversely, the bottom of the market (or pullback stage) is defined by feelings of anger, depression and disbelief. Investors grapple with these heavy emotions and believe the bull market will never return. But there is a positive: this is considered the point of maximum financial opportunity.

This is what's known as being a contrarian, and it's essential for managing emotions in crypto.

I encourage all new investors to become familiar with this chart and learn to recognise the emotional patterns that accompany these cycles. This is going to help you make more educated guesses and allow for a more disciplined and informed approach to investing.

2. The Fear and Greed Index

This is another great tool for analysing the sentiment of the global market. It takes into account various factors, including volatility, market momentum, trading volume and social media sentiment. At one end of the index we have extreme fear, while greed sits at the other.

Here's an example of what it looked like in 2023 at the start of a bull market.[10]

As you can see, the fear is low, and the greed is increasing slowly. But just a few months prior to this, everything was in the red.

Group sentiment can change rapidly. As smart investors, we want to avoid groupthink, be strategic, remain in charge of our emotions and stay ahead of the crowd.

So, what can you do with the information these tools provide? You have a choice. You can be a textbook investor who follows the sentiment of the crowd and allows your emotions to dictate your investment choices. Not advised.

Or you can be a *contrarian* and use these tools as an indicator of when to enter and exit this market. Be mindful of the emotions that arise but don't let them influence your decisions.

Now let's look at our biggest indicator for what the overall market is doing.

Chapter 11

Bitcoin Is Your Key Indicator

Crypto's magic lies in its simplicity.
It's an asset class like no other, yet it's overshadowed by fear
of the unknown.

In the crypto world, one cryptocurrency indicates the health of the market overall, and that is *Bitcoin*.

Bitcoin is known as the reserve cryptocurrency, much like USD has become the reserve fiat currency. Whatever happens with Bitcoin has a flow-on effect on the broader crypto market, so following the price of Bitcoin and its previous cycles will give us valuable information on when to enter this market safely. When Bitcoin climbs and begins to approach its new all-time high, it triggers the remaining market to start moving, beginning with Ethereum, and followed by other coins and projects.

As a new investor, understanding Bitcoin is key to your timing of the market and the kinds of results you can expect to gain. We don't actually need to track a whole lot of cryptocurrencies; we can just look at Bitcoin to predict what the entire market's next moves might be. Understanding these market cycles is like having a backstage pass to the entire show. Once you have this simple skill, you can time your market entry like a pro.

In the next few chapters, I'll be tracing Bitcoin's history to give you the ultimate insight into crypto market cycles and super cycles. When you combine this with your understanding of human emotions and market sentiment, you can supercharge your success like never before!

Chapter 12

Super Cycles: Look to the Past, to Know the Future

Let the market do the heavy lifting for you.

Super cycles mark extraordinary phases of growth and evolution in the crypto landscape. They propel Bitcoin through highs and lows and mark important stages of the journey. But there's a key element every investor needs to know about when looking at super cycles—the crucial importance of timing.

You see, buying crypto isn't like buying a car or a piece of jewellery, meaning you shouldn't just enter this market at any old time. In my opinion, you need to enter at the *right time within the cycle.* How do we know when that is? We look to the past for clues. So, let's take a trip down memory lane, back to the creation of Bitcoin in 2008.

As I mentioned earlier, Bitcoin is our key indicator for the entire market, so when we trace the Bitcoin price patterns, what we're really doing is gaining information about the crypto market as a whole. In fact, we're looking for a distinct pattern that looks a little like this:

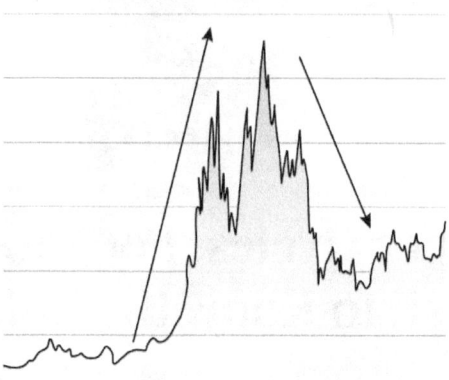

Can you see how it's denoted by a long rally upwards followed by a downward trend? This is what's known as a super cycle. When you understand this pattern, you can time your entry and prosper in this market every time. Knowing about super cycles is like having a head start on the market. It's crucial for the level of success we want.

Let's take a closer look at five of the past super cycles and the types of gains investors have made:

Super Cycle #1:

The first super cycle took place between 2010 and 2011 and gave investors up to 42,185% gains as Bitcoin went from 0.07c USD to approximately $29 USD. That's enough to turn a $100 USD investment into $42,185 USD.

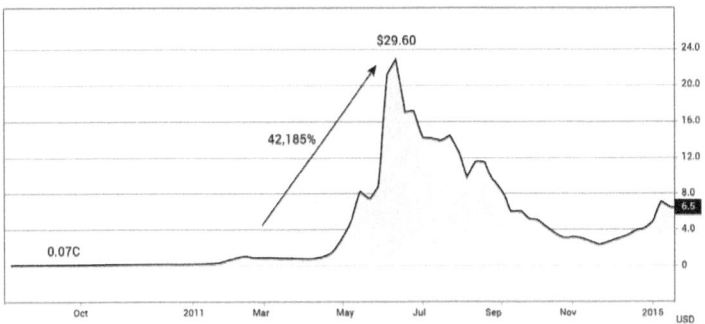

In the months following this high, Bitcoin corrected 92% and the price dropped from approximately $29 USD to $2 USD per coin.

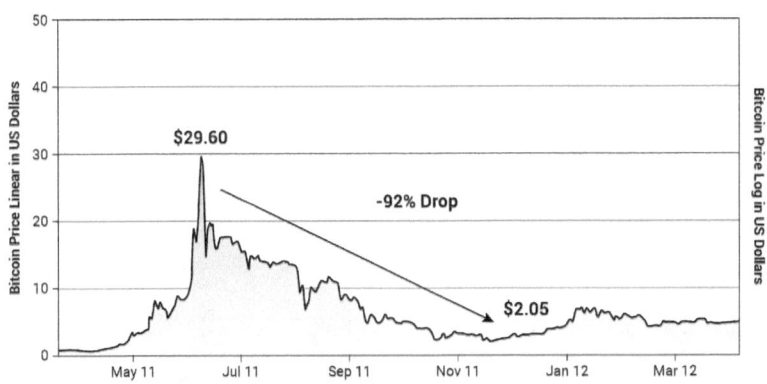

Super Cycle #2:

The second super cycle pattern took place between 2012 and 2013 and gave investors up to 5,963% gains as Bitcoin surged from around $2 USD per coin to over $140 USD per coin.

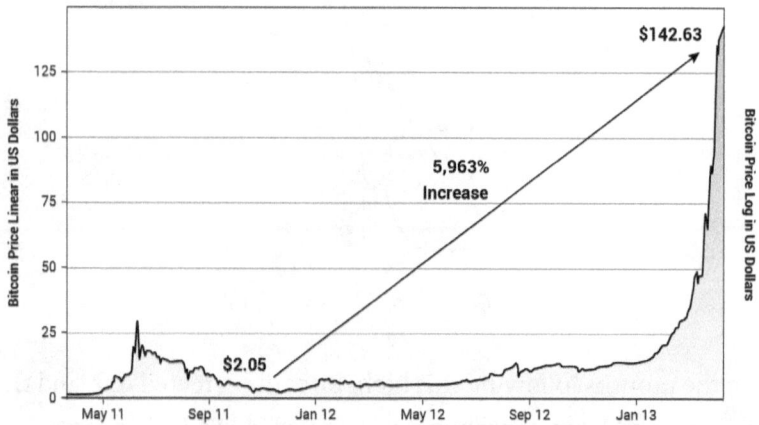

It was then followed by a market pullback of approximately 53% as Bitcoin dropped from just over $140 USD to under $70 USD per coin.

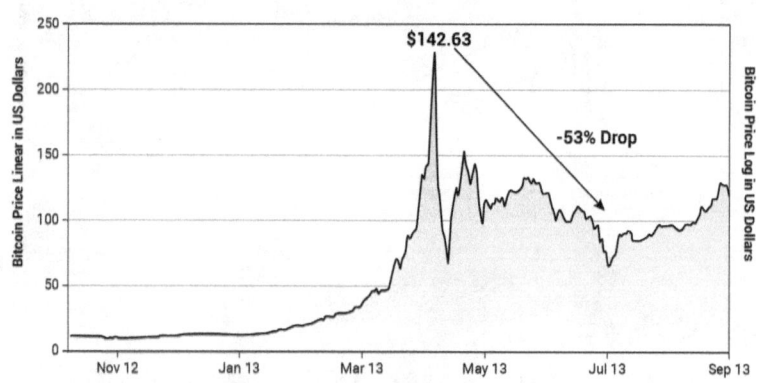

Super Cycle #3:

It wasn't long before the third super cycle arrived and Bitcoin surged from around $66 USD per coin to over $1,100 USD. This resulted in a huge 1,580% growth in the value of Bitcoin for investors.

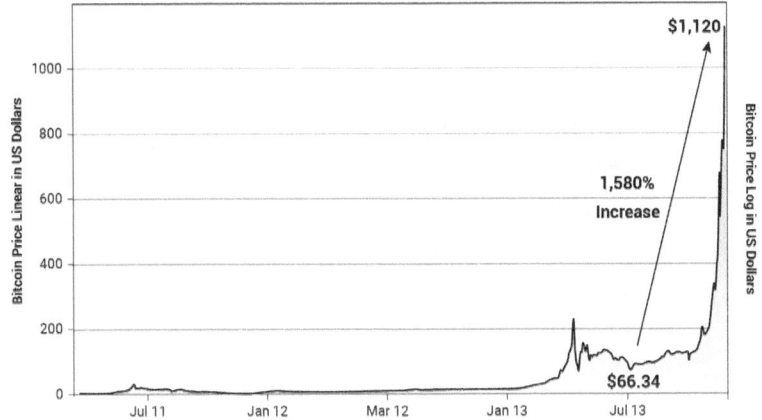

As cycles will be cycles, we saw Bitcoin correct 81%, dropping the price from $1,100 USD to around $210 USD per coin.

Super Cycle #4:

Then we get to 2017, the year that put Bitcoin on the map. Crypto had reached a level of global adoption and everyone thought Bitcoin was going to the moon and never coming down. Investors were even purchasing Bitcoin as Christmas presents and new people were drawn into the hype and euphoria surrounding it.

Unfortunately, many of them rode the wave all the way back down.

The fourth super cycle pattern played out and Bitcoin surged from just over $200 USD to as high as approximately $19,500 USD (depending on which exchange you looked at). This gave investors a 9,052% return.

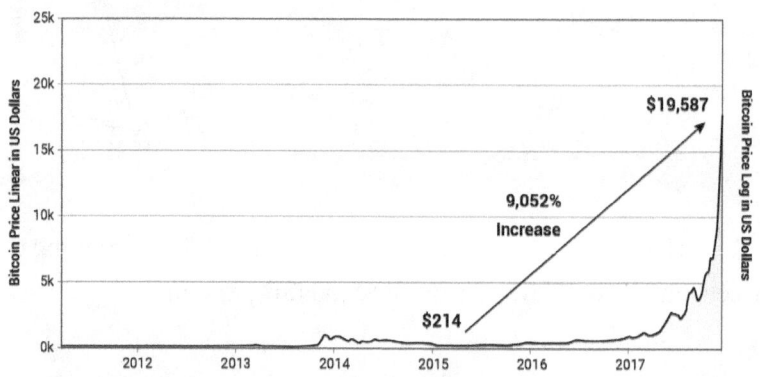

As to be expected in cycles, we saw Bitcoin correct as much as 84% as the price dropped from almost $19,500 USD to as low as $3,200 USD.

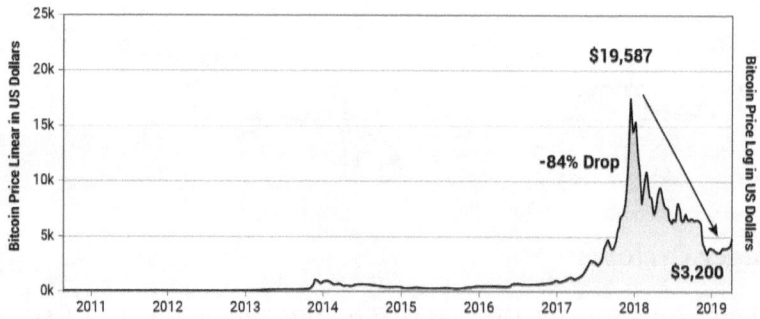

It was a low point for many new investors who followed the hype and bought at the top. But for those who thought like a contrarian, it was the ultimate turning point.

The Day We Ran a Crypto Event at the Bottom of the Market

I remember the day Bitcoin bottomed to $3,200 USD because we were running a free educational event that very weekend. My brother and I were all set to share our knowledge about this exciting new sector. But we now had a few problems: the price had plummeted, media was rife with negative coverage and the general sentiment was pessimistic.

It wasn't the best time to be holding live crypto presentations.

However, rather than cancel, we went ahead with the event and spoke about being a contrarian for two full days, morning to night. Yes, the market had dropped, but most of the wealth in crypto is acquired during those conditions. While some audience members couldn't understand the message because of media FUD (fear, uncertainty and doubt), there were many who heard us loud and clear. Some invested hundreds of thousands of dollars into Bitcoin between when it was $3,200 USD and $3,500 USD.

Where do you think these investors stand financially today?

> **The Lesson**
>
> Don't listen to mainstream FUD about crypto.
> Instead, use timing and market cycles to
> your advantage.

Now, I'm not saying that Bitcoin is the coin we all need to be rushing out and buying today, because today's market is very different to what we experienced in 2018. But I am saying that adopting a contrarian mindset will always place more upside potential in front of you than chasing the hype.

Later, I discuss new and emerging growth sectors that are yet to go through their first cycle. I call it the second wave through Crypto.

Super Cycle #5:

And then we have the super cycle pattern of 2021, where Bitcoin climbed from its previous all-time low of $3,200 USD to as high as $65,000 USD. This gave investors a return of almost 2,000% on their money, had they bought the bottom and sold close to the top.

To put that in perspective, that's a twenty-fold increase in your money in around three years.

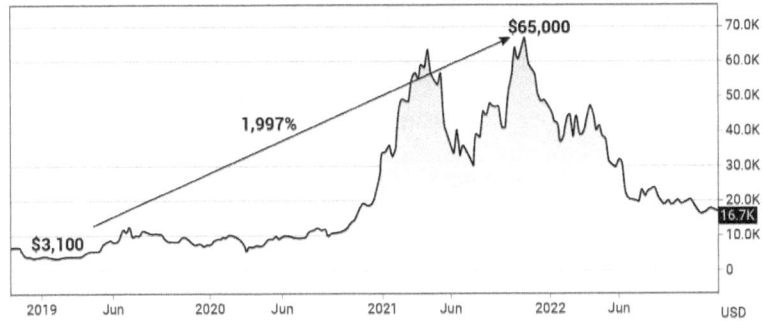

By now you've probably guessed what's coming—a big old market pullback. After November 2021, we entered the bear market and saw Bitcoin drop as low as 75% from $65,000 USD per coin to approximately $15,700 USD per coin.

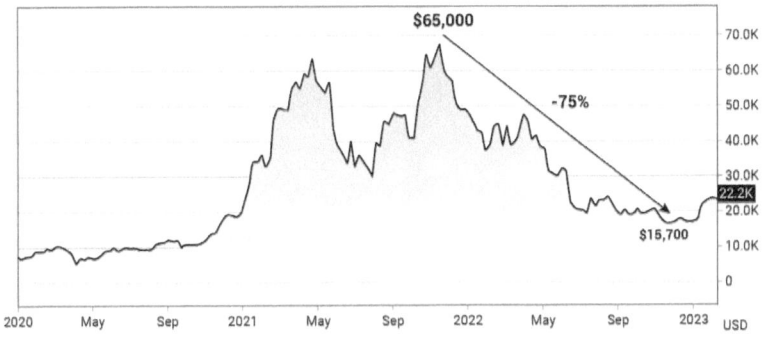

As you can see with all of these super cycles, they abide by one fundamental truth of the crypto market:

What goes up must come down.

The great thing about these patterns is that they're not just a snapshot of the past. They can act as a playbook for the future, too. Why? Because this pattern will continue to repeat itself over the lifespan of this market and every market out there. These super cycles are like clockwork. They show up again, and again, and again. And when we know what's coming, we can plan our moves and place maximum upside potential in front of us.

In other words, we can let the market do the heavy lifting for us.

Now that we understand this key pattern, let's discuss how to time our entry into it.

Chapter 13

How to Time Your Entry Like a Pro

You <u>must</u> understand where you are in the market cycle.

So, we've seen the historical gains investors have made by timing the market. Now let's look at how we can apply this knowledge to enter the market today.

Based on history, an investor who follows the right procedures and market timing could potentially expect to 10x their portfolio every market cycle. That's how I turned $20,000 into $200k, 2M, you get the idea. This is how impactful timing your entry can be. I truly believe it's one of the most important skills you can learn before investing your dollars and can be the difference between creating financial freedom or sitting on major losses for years to come.

Many new investors have been burnt by skipping this step to follow the hype and sentiment of the masses. But we are going to do things the smart way, not the hard way. So, let's dive deeper into market timing by dissecting a crypto super cycle and the four distinct zones within it. I'll break each one down and give you the indicators so you can identify where you are in the cycle today.

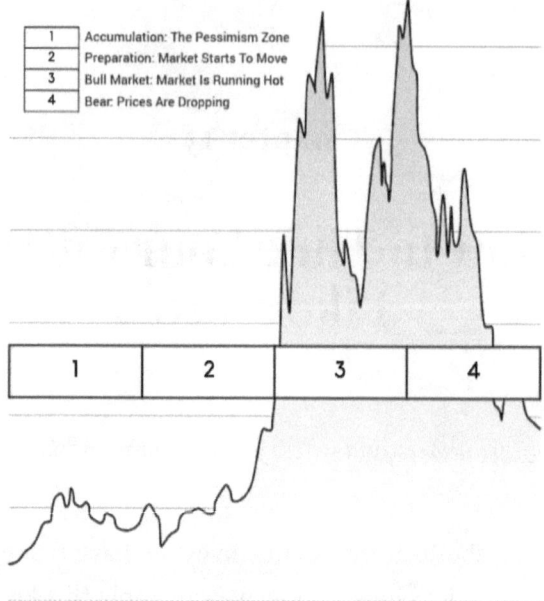

Image Source: Stock Money Lizards (Twitter)

Zone 1: Accumulation – The Pessimism Zone

Negative sentiment comes with a silver lining.

The accumulation phase typically occurs after the bear market has set in—anger and depression are rife within the community and new investors simply don't believe a bull market could ever return. This phase is also referred to as crypto winter and you can imagine why: it's known to be miserable, cold and depressing.

The accumulation phase is often denoted by Bitcoin sitting at all-time lows, negative media coverage and minimal activity on crypto social media channels. You may even find the top influencers talking about selling and 'getting out forever'. It's not unusual to see an 80-90% retracement in your portfolio at this time. The pain is real and should never be underestimated.

However, every dark cloud has a silver lining and historically, this has always been the best time to accumulate and build your positions. For investors with access to free capital, this phase can be a buying frenzy. Many millionaires are made from accumulating the most popular cryptocurrencies at major discounts during this time, as well as new ones coming to market. These savvy investors are contrarians, acting in direct opposition to group think.

Zone 2: Preparation – Market Starts to Move

Investors wait years for moments like these in the crypto cycle.

The preparation phase, also coined the 'disbelief' phase, is interestingly a period of hope and excitement. We've just come out of a gruelling crypto winter and many are still grappling with feelings of negativity and despondence. New investors don't believe the bull market is returning, but experienced investors can identify the hope that this time signifies. They start to pile up at the sidelines waiting for positive news to emerge.

During this time, the sentiment can change from negative to positive in a matter of days, sometimes even hours, and continue to flip back and forth until a positive global sentiment is established. This phase is also known as the 'pre-bull' phase because investors have read the cues and are preparing for the bull market to officially take off!

So, should we be thinking about buying during this time? In my opinion, yes. The preparation phase offers the last chance to pick up cryptocurrencies at bargain prices, with top coins and projects sitting on major discounts of 70-95%.

Zone 3: Bull Market – Market Is Running Hot

The best skill to master during a bull market is selling, not buying.

This is the moment we've all been waiting for.

It's a time when you can't scroll through social media without a crypto meme popping up. It's when your grandma is asking about Bitcoin, and your local barista is giving you stock advice. Crypto fever is everywhere, and euphoria is riding high.

A bull market presents itself only once every few years. We've experienced them in 2011, 2013, 2017, 2021 and so forth … you get the idea.

If you have investments that are already sitting in the market when this zone hits, congratulations, this is your time to shine! Enjoy it and remember not to let greed cloud your judgment when it's time to reap profits. Finding the right moment to withdraw can be a mind game. Staying realistic about your gains is key. In the upcoming chapters, I share a number of strategies for taking profit during a bull market.

And if you're new to the market and have never invested before? This is a time to exercise caution. Buying now is likely to limit the upside potential in front of you, which is the opposite of what we want to do. The best success in crypto comes when we can buy close to the bottom and sell close to the top. Anything else and we run the risk of sitting on losses.

Buying the top often does nothing but lock in losses.

Now, I know what you're thinking. 'Can I invest at all during the bull market?' The answer is, potentially, but it comes with more risk. While many coins will be sitting at all-time highs, there will be some smaller cap (newer and more speculative) coins that are ready to take off towards the end of the bull market. More on this in the next chapter.

Another thing to consider when entering during this time is to understand who is in the ring with you. In other words, will you be buying into a coin where large investors who hold substantial amounts have already made their money. If they invested well, they're probably sitting on huge gains and are just waiting for the right moment to sell.

You don't want to be their exit liquidity.

I suggest that if you're a new investor thinking about entering during a bull market, you do so very tentatively. As we know from the Wall Street Cheat Sheet, euphoria is high and sentiment is overwhelmingly positive during this time, but that doesn't make it the right time to enter crypto? Yes, there are gains to be made, but you will want to play it right and know exactly what you are doing. Remember, we want to place maximum upside potential in front of us, not downside.

So, how do we know the bull market is coming to an end? Because cryptos will be experiencing record prices with no healthy pullbacks. There's a slang term for this called the 'blow off phase'. It's where high-risk plays on speculative coins can sometimes pay off, and people are making 1,000x to 10,000x gains on silly meme coins with barely any utility. More on this in the next chapter.

Zone 4: Bear Market – Prices Are Dropping

What goes up, must come down.

As we've witnessed with the super cycle patterns, what goes up must come down and this is often the last chance to take a little more profit off the table before the market fully capitulates. This phase is probably one of the hardest parts of the journey, particularly for new investors.

The party is over and there's only one way to go now, and that is down.

Zone 4 marks the beginning of a potentially long bear market and a crypto winter, but the buying opportunities don't really present themselves until the *end of this zone*. This can catch investors off guard and test their emotional resilience. As prices nosedive, panic sets in because people just can't believe this is happening. This prompts a frenzied scramble to grab any profits that remain.

This phase is also known as the 'tear your hair out' phase of the market to new investors—particularly those who entered crypto at the top of the bull market phase. (This won't be true for seasoned investors who know the cycles and took profits along the way.) The key to getting through it is to be patient and keep your emotions in check. Understand that this is a natural part of crypto, the tide *will* turn, and the buying (and selling) opportunities will present themselves again.

Remember, the cyclical movements of cryptocurrencies allow us to strategically enter and exit the market to create life-changing wealth. In my opinion, if you're lucky enough to discover crypto during the end of this phase, you'll be presented with the greatest buying opportunity of your lifetime! And if you've missed the boat this time around? Don't worry because the cycle will start again.

> *"If you think you missed the boat because prices keep pumping, remember the market will always pull back and present you an opportunity to enter."*
>
> **Coach Michael, Digital Wealth Group**

Outside investors look at the volatility of crypto and despise it, but established investors and those learning about it for the first time can't get enough. We know that the volatility from cyclical changes in the market is our best opportunity for a potential early retirement—when done right.

I believe crypto is actually a simple game, but many overcomplicate it with emotions and illogical reasoning. They listen to mass media rather than learning about market cycles. So, delay your gratification, choose your market timing and know that spending the right amount of time in the market will put maximum upside in front of you.

Crypto will always favour the bold and the patient, so stay savvy and play the long game. Ultimately, the potential for retirement in three to four years is well worth the wait.

"The intelligent investor is a realist who sells to optimists and buys from pessimists."

Benjamin Graham

Chapter 14

Inside a Bull Market

Make this bull market your market.

Now that we've learned about the four market zones, I want to zoom in and dissect one zone in particular, and that is the beloved bull market. Why? Because there are key events that occur within it that you need to be aware of. You see, each bull market has certain events we can use as guideposts. They indicate where we are in the bull market and allow us to navigate more effectively. As always in crypto, we want to use knowledge over emotions to make informed, strategic decisions.

Here are the key bull market events, based on every previous cycle so far.

Key Event 1: Bitcoin Leads the Way

Historically, Bitcoin is the first crypto to take off in price, signalling the very early beginnings of the bull market. We'll see Bitcoin approach or even break through its previous all-time high and this can happen across a few short months, sometimes even weeks. Up until this moment, Bitcoin has typically been outperforming the remainder of the market.

Key Event 2: Ethereum's Turn

As Bitcoin starts to draw international attention and billions of dollars to the asset class once again, we'll see the second largest cryptocurrency, Ethereum, start to move. It's been predicted by some analysts that Ethereum will briefly overtake Bitcoin to become the top cryptocurrency in terms of market capitalisation and percentage growth (note, this doesn't mean value). This event has been coined 'the flippening' in crypto communities.

Key Event 3: Large Cap Cryptos Step In

Once Bitcoin and Ethereum have reached their new all-time highs (or are on their way there), it's not uncommon for the larger cap crypto's to start to rise in value. These include your top thirty to fifty cryptos by any aggregator website. This is mainly due to the fact that so much capital is pouring into this space, and this has an on-flow effect to the broader market. Generally speaking, what's good for Ethereum and Bitcoin is good for the entire market.

In other words *'a rising tide lifts all boats"*.

Key Event 4: Small Cap Meme Season Marks the Near End

Once the larger cap cryptos are moving, it's not uncommon for the smaller cap cryptos to now move—and fast.

On the market cap list, any coin or project ranked fifty or below is generally considered a smaller cap crypto. They represent a more speculative sector of the market. As a general rule of thumb, the lower the market cap, the easier to experience multiple percent gains because it takes only a small amount of capital to move the price. Why is this important? Because when we near the end of a bull market, we'll see these small cap cryptos take off in price. This is known as the final phase of the bull market, as it's often where you see investors making astronomical gains from novelty meme coins with dogs or frogs on them. The euphoria is high to say the least.

In summary, here's how we could expect a bull market to play out, based on history:

Bitcoin: The start of the bull market is indicated by Bitcoin increasing in price, typically within a short timeframe.

Ethereum: Ethereum will begin to take off when Bitcoin approaches its previous all-time high.

Large Caps: The top thirty to fifty cryptocurrencies will begin to increase in value after Ethereum starts to perform.

Small Caps: Lastly, small cap cryptos (ranked fifty and below) will begin to rapidly increase in value, indicating the end of the bull market is close.

So, there you have it, a full snapshot of market cycles and how to time your entry to place maximum upside potential in front of you.

Chapter 15

Crypto Investing: It's a Plan, Within a Plan, Within a Plan

There are many lenses through which we can view the crypto market and each one offers something of value.

I hope you enjoyed uncovering the key crypto investing secrets that will drive the market to all new heights. As you can see, there are many factors that come into play when doing crypto the right way and making smart, informed investment choices. It's about building your knowledge and elevating your understanding so you can amplify your wealth-building potential. Some would say crypto investing is like having a plan, within a plan … within a plan. In other words, there are many layers to what drives this market.

Let's review what we've just learned. We can:

- Examine human sentiment and emotions, recognising that one of the most underrated drivers of the market is the sentiment of the mass crowd.

- Identify the four zones of the market and where we sit within them. Are we at the start of a bull market or on the way out of one?
- Time our entry based on market zones (I believe this is more important than the actual coins you buy).
- Recognise when the bull market is in full swing by the natural flow of capital from top cryptos like Bitcoin and Ethereum down to the broader speculative and large cap alt coins.

Understanding the core concepts introduced here in Part 2 will have you miles ahead of the crowd and entering the market like a professional, placing as much upside in front of you as possible.

In Part 3, we're going to take action and begin building our crypto portfolio the right and safe way.

Let's Hear from Our Students

Timothy
Paraburdoo, Western Australia

"I used to work in the mining industry in Western Australia and heard about the gains that people were making in Bitcoin. I had absolutely no idea where to start, and I wasn't very computer literate, but I reached out to Aden and Sydel from DWG, as I used to work with Aden in the mines. They took me through everything I needed to know and helped me with my first trade.

My first investment into Bitcoin was $20,000 AUD and within three weeks, it had turned into $44,500 AUD, so $24,500 in profits alone. I ended up cashing it out to help *a friend in need, but it wasn't long until I came back.*

I began dollar cost averaging into Bitcoin, moving $140,000 over the course of six months. Each month, I invested $23,300 into the market, regardless of the price. I ended up buying Bitcoin for $5,600, $8,200, $6,800, $6,500, $3,700, and $4,400, which averaged out to $5,866 per Bitcoin.

Over the next few months, Bitcoin went up to $13,700, which meant I well and truly doubled my investment. As soon as that happened, I removed my initial $140,000 capital, so I was trading with the remaining $140,000 AUD, which was pure profits. All of this happened within an eight-month window. I then held that $140,000 profit in the market and grew it to $700,000 in the next bull market. I cashed out my entire position at this point and it was a life-changing experience I'll never forget. I intend to get back into the market again soon."

Loraine, 57
Brisbane, Australia

"My most significant success in the world of cryptocurrency has been turning an initial investment of $1,875 into a substantial portfolio valued at over $210,000 today. This remarkable financial growth has opened up new possibilities and financial security for my future.

My cryptocurrency endeavours have provided me with a promising source of income, which is helping me work towards my future aspirations."

PH2M
Melbourne, Australia

"Since delving into the world of cryptocurrency, my investments have experienced remarkable growth. Some projects I've been involved in have surged by 10x, 100x, or even an astounding 10,000x in just a short one and a half years. This incredible financial growth, however, is just one facet of the journey.

What's truly exciting is how these crypto investments have helped me achieve life-changing milestones. I've witnessed my portfolio expand exponentially, which has given me newfound financial security and the potential to retire comfortably. This remarkable journey has not only reshaped my financial future but also deepened my understanding of cryptocurrency's pivotal role in reshaping the global economy.

But the impact extends beyond my own life. Inspired by these crypto successes, I've had the privilege of introducing friends and family to this transformative world of possibilities. Together, we're exploring the potential of cryptocurrency to secure financial freedom and create brighter futures."

PART THREE

Create Your Portfolio And Make It Work For You

Now it's time to build your crypto portfolio, the safe way *and* the right way.

With so many options in this market, it can be hard to know where to start, let alone which cryptocurrencies to purchase. So, in this section, you'll discover the basics to building your seven-figure crypto portfolio (and beyond).

I'll share with you:

- The tried-and-tested safety measures that will keep your assets secure.
- Key questions to ask when deciding which cryptocurrencies to invest in.
- The exact number of coins you should hold for optimum growth.
- My top performing growth sectors and how to profit from the next major wave coming to crypto.
- One of my top DWG crypto investing playbooks that many of my students used to turn $20,000 into almost $500,000 in just twelve months.
- The key secrets to make your portfolio work for you and safely create an extra passive income of $500-$1,500 per week.

You've learned when to enter the market, what happens in a bull market and the role human emotions play. Now you'll learn exactly how to enter this market in a way that is strategic and safe. I'll share the proven pathways that ensure your crypto entry isn't just a gamble, it's a well-calculated step toward a potentially very lucrative future.

Remember, crypto rewards those that do it right and play the patience game. Read every step carefully as I have hand-selected the key pieces of information you need to know and cut out the unnecessary.

Let's begin.

Key Terms & Translations

In this chapter we talk about:

Private Keys / Seed Phrase / Keys: A collection of words that act as the key to your crypto.

Portfolio: Your personal collection of cryptocurrencies that you own.

Wallet: A device, app or website that allows you to view your crypto.

Exchange: An online platform where you buy crypto with fiat currency, or swap one crypto for another.

Centralised Exchange: An exchange with a middleman, run by a third party.

Decentralised Exchange: A peer-to-peer exchange run by a decentralised application with no middleman.

Liquidity: The amount of buying and selling activity happening with that crypto.

Pump: Crypto prices go up in value, typically very fast.

Dump: Crypto prices drop rapidly in value.

Chapter 16

Private Keys and the Golden Rule of Crypto

Not your keys, not your crypto.

Throughout this book, I mention 'private keys' a number of times, so let's get into why they're so important.

Private keys are also known as your seed phrase. It's most commonly a series of either twelve or twenty-four unrelated words that are listed in order. How do you get a set of these keys? They are automatically generated when you establish your own crypto wallet (more on wallets in the next chapter). These keys are the access codes to your crypto and the one thing that guarantees *you* are in control of your funds. Holding your keys is everything when it comes to crypto, and I can't stress this enough. In fact, this is *the* number one golden rule for keeping your crypto assets safe.

"Never ever trust someone on the Internet with important personal information or security keys to your crypto. <u>Never!</u>"
Coach Jeremy, Digital Wealth Group

It's absolutely essential to protect your private keys and keep them safe at all times. Scammers will try to extract your keys from you, and they can be very creative about how they do it. But you never need to share them with anyone. In fact, the only time you need to enter your private keys is when you're restoring a wallet from scratch. That's it! You don't need them to confirm a transaction or verify your identity or to buy or sell crypto.

So how do you keep your private keys safe? Here are my top three tips.

Tip #1 Never Take a Photo of Your Private Keys

Most of us have camera rolls that are like storage vaults for personal data. But when it comes to your private keys, taking a photo of them is one thing you don't want to do. Why? Because malware-infected apps are everywhere! Any app you've downloaded to your phone could present a risk of malicious software that is programmed to trawl through a photo gallery looking for listed words, aka your private keys. I've actually heard of people who have had their wallets drained in this way. To avoid this happening, simply refrain from taking photos of your seed phrase or any other sensitive information related to your crypto assets.

Tip #2 Store Your Keys Offline

It's best to keep your private keys away from the Internet, email and technology altogether. Write them on a piece of paper, laminate them and store them in a waterproof bag or fireproof safe. Or better yet, opt for an indestructible, high-quality steel plate that you punch your seed phrase into.

Mark from Perth, Western Australia Uses Eco Safe Ink

A DWG student, Mark, was new to crypto investing when he decided to purchase his first hardware wallet. He followed all the right steps to record his private keys, except for one minor detail—he used a pen with biodegradable ink. Months later, he went to crosscheck his private keys against his hardware wallet only to find the series of words had vanished. His private keys had literally disintegrated in the heat within the safe. Luckily for Mark, he could still access his wallet and move those funds over to a new wallet with a new set of private keys.

The Lesson

Always use a pen to record your private keys, or better yet, use a steel plate so you never have to worry about natural disasters getting in the way.

Tip #3 Test Your Seed Phrase

Your hardware wallet comes with a desktop app that allows you to check and verify the validity of your seed phrase. Once you've recorded your seed phrase for the first time, you can double check it using this app. If you've had the same wallet for a long time, it may be worth going through this process at least once to verify that your private keys are correctly recorded. This one extra safety measure can potentially save a lot of grief in the future.

Serra's Potential $12,000,000 Disaster

Serra, a student from 2017, had accumulated a large amount of crypto over the years. She held three different hardware wallets all stored in the same vault. After moving house a few times, she thought it was a good idea to check that her private keys matched each associated wallet. At the time, she was holding over $12 million AUD in cryptocurrencies (from a total capital investment of $70,000 AUD). It turns out her private keys did not match the devices because she'd mixed them up during the move. We helped her to reorganize her funds and establish the wallets with their correct keys.

The Lesson

Had one of her wallets been corrupted, there's a high chance she would have lost part of her $12 million.
A critical oversight with potentially devastating consequences.

Cryptocurrencies give us the ability to be our own bank and the power to create our own wealth. But with great power comes great responsibility. There is no 'forgotten password' button if you happen to lose your crypto keys, and if someone else gets hold of them, it's game over. That's why implementing these measures and taking full responsibility for your private keys is paramount to a safe crypto journey.

Next, let's look at the other crucial component for keeping your crypto safe: wallets.

Chapter 17

Crypto Wallets and Storing Your Digital Wealth

The only way to truly own crypto is to own the private key in a wallet you control.
Anything else is simply an IOU.

So, you're ready to buy crypto, but where will you store it? Well, just as you hold money in a wallet in the physical world, you hold crypto in a wallet in the digital world. The wallet you choose will have a direct impact on the safety and security of your crypto assets, so it's essential to choose wisely.

The first key thing to know about wallets is that there are two types:

Hot = connected to the Internet.
Cold = not connected to the Internet.

There are pros and cons to each, but only one of them has superior security.

Hot wallets are convenient and accessible—all you need is an Internet connection and you're good to go. Most centralised exchanges have free hot wallets as part of their platform, and when you buy crypto, they automatically get stored there. But be warned, when your crypto is in a wallet on an exchange, you won't own the private keys to these wallets—the exchange will. Even though an exchange wallet is attached to your name and account, it's the private keys that dictate ownership.

Keeping money in an exchange wallet (which translates to leaving money on the exchange you purchased it from) is very convenient. But it isn't safe because we're essentially handing over the responsibility for the security of our funds to that exchange. This is why I say exchanges need to be treated like shopping malls—a place to make purchases, but never leave our shopping bags there. I recommend moving funds off the exchange to a wallet in your control, where you own the private keys.

Which brings us to the superior option for keeping your crypto safe—cold wallets.

Cold wallets are also known as hardware wallets. They offer the greatest form of security and are almost impossible to hack. Cold wallets are small, USB-sized devices that hold your crypto offline. When you want to transact, you simply plug the device into your computer, move your crypto around, then unplug it again. At Digital Wealth Group, we strongly recommend cold wallets to our students because it's the only way you can 100% guarantee that your crypto is yours. Think of it as the Fort Knox of your digital fortune.

"Don't get lazy and never let your guard down—at the end of the day everything comes down to operational security."

Coach Alex, Digital Wealth Group

If you're in crypto for the long term, and want to be a serious investor, begin your journey the right way with cold storage methods.

Chapter 18

Choosing the Right Exchange to Buy Your Crypto

Exchanges are a touch point, a shopping experience.
They are not the place you store your crypto.

So, you've got the wallet, and you understand how to keep your private keys safe. The next stop is registering on an exchange so that you can purchase cryptocurrencies.

An exchange is an online platform where you swap your dollars for crypto (a process called onramping). Once you're registered and set up as a user, you can deposit funds from your bank account to your exchange account to buy crypto. It's important to choose the right exchange for you because some are user friendly, and others can be intimidating for a beginner. You want to look for an exchange with a good reputation, that has been around a long time and is simple to use.

The other thing to consider about exchanges is the location. I know what you're thinking. *'Why does the location of the exchange matter if they're all online?'* Mostly, it doesn't. But if you're just starting out and you need assistance, having someone in your time zone who speaks your language on the other end of the phone can be reassuring.

When you're setting yourself up on an exchange, there are a number of security measures you'll need to go through, including the typical KYC (Know Your Customer) protocols of sharing your passport or driver's license. It can feel like you're giving away a lot of personal information when you register for an exchange, but unfortunately this is the process we need to go through to get verified. As long as you're using a legitimate exchange, there's nothing to worry about. Also, remember we aren't going to keep our crypto here long term. This is simply the shopping expedition before we transfer our assets to a secure wallet.

Now, when you first join an exchange, you'll be limited as to how much crypto you can buy each day. For example, many exchanges impose a daily deposit limit of around $2,000 per day. If you want to increase it, you'll need to go through the tedious process of being verified for this by the exchange.

So, should you start your verification process as soon as you've chosen an exchange? I would say yes, it's a great idea. Why? Because if you want to invest a large amount quickly, and you don't have your prior approvals in place, you potentially have a wait on your hands while you get verified. This can take anywhere from one to two days to several weeks. You could have a similar situation with your bank, so check those limits as well.

My tip. Consider registering on a few exchanges in advance, even if you don't use them yet. Different exchanges have different cryptocurrencies, and you want to be ready when opportunity comes knocking.

But perhaps the most important thing you need to know about

exchanges is that they should never be considered a safe place to keep your crypto long term. Exchanges are only to be treated as a touch point and once you've made your transactions, you can move your crypto into a wallet that *you* control, where you own the private keys.

So, what does it cost to use these exchanges?

Well, all exchanges charge a fee for transacting and, like most things in life, you pay extra for convenience. Slightly higher fees aren't necessarily a bad thing, particularly when you're starting out and you need a convenient, beginner-friendly exchange to make your life easier. Once you build up confidence, or if you wish to invest larger amounts, you can consider a cheaper exchange for some of your transactions.

Susan Accidently Paid Almost $30,000 in Fees

During the 2017 bull run, Susan, a client from Melbourne, was setting up her exchange account and had $5,000 AUD. She wanted to get in fast, without the bother of researching the right exchange and comparing fees. She figured the difference in fees could only be a few dollars, anyway. She used an exchange called Bitcoin Australia that at the time charged a fee of 5%. This meant she lost $250 in fees simply by taking a shortcut. She invested in a crypto called NEO and her investment went up 11,000% in under ninety days. Her $4,750 investment grew to $522,500. She calculated that the $250 she paid in fees could have grown to a value of around $27,500 (every $1 = $110). A bitter pill to swallow for being hasty. In reality, she could have paid a maximum of between 0.1-1.0%.

The Lesson

Take the time to choose the right crypto exchange because when you're dealing with large sums, you could save thousands.

Now let's talk liquidity.

In simple terms, liquidity reflects how easily we can trade a cryptocurrency for cash or another digital asset. High liquidity means lots of trading activity and plenty of buyers and sellers, which is something we want to look for when choosing an exchange. This gives us more options when it comes to trading or cashing out our investments.

Let's say you invest $100,000 on a coin and it does a 10x, something which is historically quite common in the crypto space. You now have $1 million in your portfolio that you want to cash out or swap for something else. In order to do that, you'll need an exchange with high liquidity so your order can be filled and your crypto successfully exchanged. In other words, you want buyers! The last thing you want is for your crypto to be sitting stagnant because your exchange doesn't have enough liquidity (enough buyers) to sell.

To summarise, when choosing the right exchange, you want to consider the following:

- Choose an exchange that makes life easy.
- Choose one in the same time zone if you think you'll need assistance.
- Convenience = higher transaction fees.
- Never keep your crypto on an exchange long term.
- Liquidity matters.

Chapter 19

Create Your First Portfolio

Your first portfolio will not be your final portfolio, so start small and work big.

Now that you've set up your wallet, stored your private keys safely, and chosen the right exchange, let's create your first crypto portfolio. In this chapter, I'll share the elements that come together to create a winning portfolio and give you a tried and tested blueprint for crypto success.

Let's start with a big mistake I see people make, and that's rushing in and taking a scatter-gun approach to acquisition. It's tempting to enter the market and load up on all the cryptos that catch your eye—a bit of this, a bit of that and the next thing you know you've accumulated sixty cryptocurrencies. That's an overwhelming number to keep track of. A smaller, well-defined and researched portfolio is much more manageable than a large one. It allows you to easily track what's happening with your coins and make smart, calculated decisions.

"If you can't briefly explain the value proposition of that Crypto, you shouldn't be buying it."

Coach Gary, Digital Wealth Group

There are literally thousands of cryptocurrencies you can buy in this diverse space. Everything from a fluffy dog coin designed to pump off the back of a social media alert and dump just as fast, to a tried and tested decentralised app that provides enormous value to the broader ecosystem. One coin has no utility and the price action is connected to social consensus and the other is valuable and helps solve real-world problems.

This is the importance of knowing the basics of what you're investing into, who's behind the project and where it's going from here.

To help you buy crypto the right way and the safe way, I've broken the creation phase down into five steps.

Step 1: Ask These Questions

With thousands of coins and projects in the crypto space, how do you know which ones are likely to be valuable? What determines value in the crypto world?

One word: utility.

The reason Bitcoin rose by more than 100,000%, or from approximately $20 to $20,000 in the five years since January 2013, is due to its underlying technology and utility—the blockchain. It's so good that due to the amount of processing power, Bitcoin is one of the strongest computing networks. Bitcoin has paved the way for many other well-designed blockchain technologies to be developed (and believe me, there are many) and each one is different in its function, development and purpose, but here's a tip:

> *If a project has good utility, it has the ability to completely disrupt many of our mainstream industries, not just finance.*

When I'm choosing coins and projects to invest in, those with the most utility and the most momentum in terms of adoption are always top of my list—before fluffy dog meme coins The more useful something is, the more longevity it has in this market.

Here are some questions to consider when you're looking at coins to invest in.

1. What is the utility of the coin or project and does it make sense?

In other words, can you tell me what this coin or project actually does? The aim here is to summarise it in one sentence. For example, a crypto that represents a brand new blockchain has a lot of utility because apps can be built on top of it. The roadmap for a new blockchain is typically enormous, so this would be considered to have strong utility.

2. How will it redefine the crypto space or create value for people?

Look for innovative features or concepts that differentiate the project from current solutions. What is the unique value proposition that this coin or project offers? For example, in DeFi you can stake your crypto to earn much better interest than you could with a bank.

3. What current industries or sectors is it promising to disrupt?

Does your crypto provide a better solution to something that currently exists? For example, is it creating more trust when it comes to voting? Or providing a simple way to take out a loan against your crypto?

4. Who is the team behind it?

How long has the team been around and what key players are working on this project? Following their social media pages will give you an idea of how active they are and what they are promising investors.

5. Is it well presented?

Is the information about this crypto presented in a clear and concise way? Does the project have a website with accurate information, or is there a lack of clarity around goals and objectives? Is the website presented well or does it lack professionalism?

Can you see how choosing your coins is much more than just a guessing game? It's wise to ask these questions and do this research before you make your crypto picks. Knowing what you're investing in creates a deeper understanding of the entire ecosystem and makes you a much better investor over time.

> *"Keeping detailed notes of your holdings, your trades/stakes and the reasoning and strategy behind them is priceless."*
>
> **Coach Alex, Digital Wealth Group**

To this day, some of the most lucrative investments I ever made came from researching and understanding the long-term value proposition of a project. One in particular had utility that was unlike anything else I'd seen, and I remember calling my colleagues to check whether I was actually interpreting it correctly because it was solving problems and providing solutions in a way that was a first for the Crypto sector.

That crypto did 10,000x in its lifetime. And that was no surprise.

Having some understanding, even at a basic level, places you miles ahead of the average crypto investor who enters the space without doing any proper research. Devoting even an hour or two to learning is time well spent that could pay lucrative dividends into the future.

Step 2: Do You Know Your Actual Risk Tolerance?

Everyone loves the crypto market when it's climbing, but it's a very different story when it's going down. That's why I teach my students to plan for market swings and know what your risk tolerance is. In other words, how will you deal with the built-in volatility?

One way to assess your risk tolerance is to choose an amount you'd like to invest, then consider how you'd feel if it dipped by 90%. If the thought fills you with dread, you're investing too much. But if you're happy to let the market do its thing and ride out the different cycles as we've discussed earlier, then that's the right investment amount for you. As one of our coaches puts it:

> *"If you're losing sleep over market volatility, you've invested too much. Think of an amount of money you could afford to lose every week without taking food off the table or a roof from over your head. That is your budget."*
>
> **Coach Gary, Digital Wealth Group**

Whenever I think about risk tolerance, I'm reminded of a new investor who put aside $50,000 for an upcoming bill. This gentleman was desperate to be involved with crypto and invested the entire amount on one cryptocurrency that he believed would go parabolic in the next month. His timing was off, and the market corrected by 90%, sending him into panic and depression instantly. What was his mistake? He didn't plan for the volatility, and he didn't properly assess his risk tolerance. This is a critical error many new investors make.

There's an important lesson here. Always assess your risk tolerance first, and never over-invest.

My tip. Start small, work big.

Starting with a smaller capital investment means that you can begin your crypto journey without the stresses. I started my crypto investing with only a few thousand dollars. I was considered a low-risk investor and very cautious. Today, I'm considered much higher risk and I invest with sums of up to six and seven figures at once. Again, I started small to play a much longer and bigger game.

Anita, International Businesswomen, Scared to Invest $300,000

It was early 2022 when I spoke with a woman who travelled internationally for work. She was extremely successful and had a net worth in the high seven figures. In our initial conversation, she expressed her concern about investing $300,000 into the market. She told me she'd been overthinking it for months. I told her she didn't need to go in so strongly. She could start with 10% of that amount and see how it felt. The relief in her voice was instantaneous. This was something she hadn't even considered—starting small and working up as her portfolio grew in value.

> ### The Lesson
> You don't have to start with a huge sum of money. You can start small and add capital to your portfolio as your confidence increases.

Step 3: How Many Coins Will You Hold?

So, if you've done your research and you're eager to buy, what is the specific number of coins you should look to hold for optimum portfolio growth?

Ten to fifteen coins. That's it!

Our most successful students and best-performing portfolios at Digital Wealth Group all have this in common. Within that number, around five of those you could expect to be permanent, long-term holds. The other five to ten will typically be traded, swapped and moved around accordingly.

> *"Don't spread your attention too thin. Smaller is better when it comes to portfolio size. This space moves quickly, and you need to stay on top of what is happening so you can react in a timely manner."*
>
> **Coach Jeremy, Digital Wealth Group**

While the scatter-gun approach can sometimes land you a fluke coin that goes parabolic, I don't recommend it as a strategy. After all, we want to create long-term, generational wealth over short-term gains.

Jane Holds 120 Cryptocurrencies

Jane, a student who joined the DWG program in 2019, originally came to us with a record amount of cryptocurrencies in her portfolio. She held 120 coins and projects with anywhere from $50-$200 invested on each one. To say it was chaos was an understatement. The storing, managing and tracking of these projects was near impossible and Jane was missing out on gains because of it. Why? Because she lost track of where things were stored, the private keys and the apps and wallets that were used to manage them all. We helped her scale them down to a manageable and profitable portfolio that she could control easily.

The Lesson

Hold a smaller, more manageable amount of cryptocurrencies and keep notes on where they are stored and how you plan to sell them or take profit.

Step 4: Deploy Your Cash

Now that you are ready to hit the buy button, how will you do it? Will you attempt to buy at the bottom and invest all of your capital at once (a risky move if you're not confident reading charts), or will you invest in smaller portions through dollar cost averaging? Perhaps you want to do a combination of both, where you invest some capital upfront, then use dollar cost averaging to invest the remainder?

Dollar cost averaging (DCA) is a strategy where you invest regular amounts of money at consistent intervals, regardless of the market and price conditions. This means investing in a bear market, a bull market and everything in between. Why do we do this? To mitigate the volatility and take the emotion out of your buying practice. If you know that every Wednesday you deposit into the market, you can reduce the time trying to track daily ups and downs. If there was ever a way to invest into the market while removing as much emotion as possible, DCA is it.

DCA looks something like this:

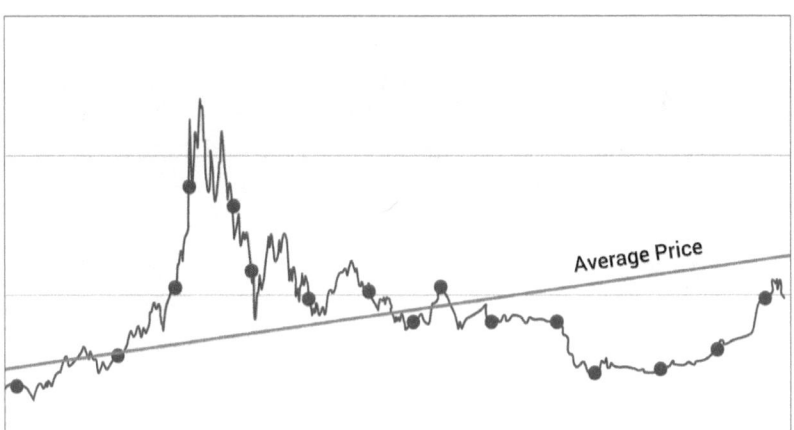

The dots represent all the regular injections of capital. You can see that it results in an average price that is possibly much lower than if you were to allocate all of your funds at once. And the best part? It removes all the stress around trying to time the market.

George Invests $100 Per Week and Returns 612% in Three Years

George, a student of DWG, purchased $100 USD of a low-risk, conservative cryptocurrency called Ethereum every week between December 2018 and 2021. The total amount he invested over three years came to $15,700 USD. He sold around three years later, and his portfolio was valued at $111,830 USD. He made a return of 612% on his money using dollar cost averaging.

> ### The Lesson
> Small, regular investing amounts over time is a smart and safe way to add to your portfolio and increase your gains.

DCA is recommended for those who are just getting started, especially in the pre-bull/preparation phase of the market. It's great if you aren't comfortable reading charts or don't want to spend excess time tracking the next market move. Some investors use DCA as a long-term savings account, either for themselves or as a future gift (for a child or grandchild as an example).

The only time DCA isn't my top recommended strategy is when we're in the midst of the crypto winter (bear market). This is a time when deploying larger amounts of capital can be a strategic move, because you're placing maximum upside potential in front of you. Much of my financial success has been made largely from investing during this time.

As you can see, knowing where you are in the cycle, as discussed in Part 2, and not overthinking your timing through DCA is a wonderful, low time commitment way to start investing. As I always say, it's better to have some skin in the game than to sit on the sidelines for fear of mis-timing the market.

Step 5: Look for Major Growth Sectors

Choosing coins and sectors to invest in can feel like searching for a needle in the haystack—there are just so many options out there. But the good news is, we don't need to play the guessing game with our crypto. We can, and should, narrow our focus to ensure we have exposure to one key thing—major growth sectors.

The reason we should include growth sectors is because they represent innovation in this space, which equates to the potential for great gains and project longevity. We should seek coins and projects that will see multiple successful cycles and bear fruit for years to come. It's a strategy that has worked time and time again, and I'll share exactly how we can construct a playbook using these growth sectors in Step 6.

When new investors feel they've missed out because they didn't invest in Bitcoin or Ethereum, I remind them of the second major wave coming through crypto, which I believe is within these top three growth sectors:

1. Decentralised Finance (DeFi)
2. New Blockchain Technology (the technical term is 'Layer 1 and Layer 2' Infrastructure)
3. The Metaverse (virtual worlds) and Gaming

These mega trends, among a few others, are set for an incredible growth trajectory over the coming decade. Understanding why and how to get our positions into them can set us up for incredible future success. Remember, it would be ludicrous to expect all the best technology for disruptive innovations to roll out on day one. Sometimes the best investment opportunities come years into the game.

So why am I so bullish on these growth sectors? Let's take a deeper look...

Growth Sector 1: DeFi – Decentralised Finance

What if I told you that the largest sector to date, finance, is about to be disrupted in a huge way? And it's not happening in the distant future—it's already started. Because that's exactly what's going on.

We already know the current frustrations:

- Slow banks
- Tedious loan processes
- Outdated and archaic systems
- Expensive fees for overseas transfers
- Bank account exploitations and hacks
- Potential bank runs
- Account limitations

- Arduous paperwork and identification processes
- Centralised control and monitoring of our transactions
- In the worst cases, being locked out of our accounts

And the list goes on.

Our legacy financial system is ripe for disruption and that's exactly what DeFi is doing. Because with DeFi, *you* are the bank. No middlemen, no paperwork, no gatekeepers, no exorbitant fees. Just you in complete control over your finances. Everything you can do in the traditional banking system, you can also do in the DeFi world. In fact, right now you can:

- Hold money in an account that only you control and see
- Borrow, lend, trade, sell and move money around privately, all in one click
- Take out a loan with 0% interest
- Produce that loan within minutes
- Earn two, three and even four figure APY yields (interest earned)
- Store money in cryptographically secure vaults
- Transfer money overseas for pennies
- Never have to use a house as collateral, supply ID or submit paperwork ever again

As you can see, revolutionary doesn't begin to explain it!

So how does it work? Well, it all comes down to code.

DeFi is executed through smart contracts, which is code that is self-executing when predefined conditions are met. We no longer need to be tied up in bureaucracy, waiting on a bank to do time-consuming checks when smart contracts do the same thing within minutes. The smart contract does all the heavy lifting and ensures the transaction goes through safely and transparently via the blockchain.

Are you starting to see the value proposition of something like this?

If you measure from 2017 to the peak of the 2021 bull market, the Total Value Locked (TVL) went from less than $100 million up to $175 billion.[11] That's a significant number of people making the move to DeFi to engage in that space.

So, how do you invest into this wonderful and game changing technology? You choose coins that are building out the infrastructure, supporting the ecosystem and reflecting the development of the growth sector that is DeFi.

Here's how that might work.

Say you invest in Coin X, which represents a lending platform where you can effortlessly borrow against your cryptocurrency in the form of a loan. By making this investment, you're not only able to use the new and disruptive technology, but you're also an early investor in its growth and trajectory. It's a little like buying stocks in Apple—it's one thing to use their computers and devices, but investing into the company's growth would have also reaped colossal rewards.

Remember, every crypto coin or project represents something—be it a company, an innovation or a game changing piece of technology. These are not just a bunch of funny names and logos. They're the infrastructure that will change our world. We've seen it happen in multibillion dollar industries before—just think of what Airbnb and Uber did to the accommodation and taxi industries. Each one got turned on its head by the introduction of 'better options'. And the finance sector is about to go through the same.

"Learn to use the amazing protocols that are being built. This really is the evolution of the financial system. You can be an investor in this space, but you can also be just a user of the technology."

Coach Jeremy, Digital Wealth Group

Now, let's move onto the next growth sector: blockchain development.

Growth Sector 2: New Blockchain Technology

New blockchain technology is represented by two things:

Layer 1 – A brand new blockchain.
Layer 2 – The scaling technology that makes an existing blockchain run better.

Now, if the words 'blockchain' and 'technology' sound a little too technical for your liking, stay with me because I'm going to break it down in the simplest of terms.

Layer 1 is basically infrastructure for the crypto ecosystem. Think of it as the railway tracks that all the trains (crypto projects) operate on top of. Ethereum is a popular Layer 1 blockchain, with thousands of cryptocurrencies that operate on top of it.

Layer 2 on the other hand, is all the technology that makes that railway operate smoothly. Think scheduling and ticketing systems, and the staff to monitor and repair it if needed. In other words, Layer 2 technology makes Layer 1 function better.

Layer 1 and Layer 2 both fall under the same category: *new blockchain technology*. Historically speaking, investing in new blockchain technology has proved to be one of the most profitable growth sectors you can get exposure to.

A study of seven new Layer 1 and Layer 2 blockchains, crypto ticker symbols AVAX, BNB, SOL, LUNA, FTM, ATOM and CELO, reported that on average, it took 1.4 years to reach an all-time high with an average return for investors of 656x on their money.

Think about that for a moment.

Based on these statistics, $100 USD (which is pretty much what a small basket of groceries costs in Australia by today's standards) could be worth $65,600 USD in 1.4 years' time.

$1,000 would turn into $656,000 USD.

$10,000 would turn into $6,560,000 USD.

Do you still think you need to break the bank to enter into crypto?

This is why we focus on major growth sectors.

You don't have to be a developer to buy into new blockchain technology. Any investor can do it. You simply hold the crypto that represents that new blockchain (where the innovation and development is) and you're up and away.

Growth Sector 3: Metaverse and Gaming

Now let's look at the fascinating and controversial world of the metaverse and gaming.

For those that don't know, the metaverse is simply a computer-generated, virtual world where a user's avatar engages with the world and has experiences. You put on the goggles, and you see a completely different reality where you can play games, socialise, attend events, interact with others, buy property and even have pets. Everything that resides within the metaverse is known as an NFT (Non-Fungible Token)—basically digital goods. NFTs can be the artwork in someone's house, the items you buy at a store, the dog that barks at you as you pass by or the shoes on your feet.

What's interesting about these digital goods is they can go for a pretty penny (all transactions in the metaverse are done mainly through digital currency (cryptocurrency). In fact, some NFTs are worth over half a billion dollars. So why do investors own these? Because there's a social consensus applied which deems them collectable and shareable. For example, a picture of a monkey with a cigarette hanging from its mouth can be deemed valuable because a celebrity displays it on the backdrop of their live show. This contributes to its status and popularity, hence it becomes highly valued. It's a bit like collectible cards back in the nineties.

Now, I know what some of you may be thinking. *'I'm not a gamer, nor do I plan to be'.* Or better yet. *'I'm not interested in virtual reality. I prefer the real world.'* And I completely understand. This is an area many people don't immediately click with. It's an unusual space and, from an ethical point of view, the metaverse rubs many people the wrong way. It can be viewed as encouraging people to disengage with the real world and immerse themselves in a fake one.

However, for the savvy investor, there's a whirlwind of opportunity here. Big money is being invested into this space, so it's not going anywhere soon. And as an undeniable growth sector, you can position yourself here for maximum gains. We always want to look at where the major growth is happening, and it's certainly within the gaming sector. In fact, Microsoft signed a 68.9 billion dollar acquisition deal in January 2022 for the gaming company Activision Blizzard—a sure sign this isn't going away anytime soon. We always want to look for projects that represent the largest growth and innovation within this sector and hold them for the long term.

Virtual real estate.

Digital goods.

Gaming and the metaverse.

These are just a few.

We don't have to interact with these virtual worlds to profit from them. We can simply invest in the companies behind the innovation and key developments of the space. This means we can profit from the growth of that company without ever putting on a headset and stepping into a virtual world (although we absolutely can do that, too, if we choose).

If history has anything to teach us, it's that gaming is about to be completely taken over by blockchain technology. It may be slow right now as games take years to develop, but in my opinion it's only a matter of time before we see record growth.

Step 6: Create a Winning Portfolio

Now, I'm going to share with you a portfolio combination straight from the Digital Wealth Group playbook. This is one of our top ten portfolios in terms of performance. It's been refined many times and proven to generate fantastic gains for our members. It focuses on high-performing growth sectors that gives us our best chance for big gains.

The great thing about these percentage breakdowns is that they can work for any amount you choose to invest, whether that's $1,000, $100,000 or anything in between. Please note that this is based on a conservative, low risk tolerance. You may like to increase or decrease certain percent allocations depending on your personal risk tolerance profile.

Here is the portfolio:
- 50% into traditional / conservative cryptocurrencies (Bitcoin and / or Ethereum)
- 21% into new blockchain technology (referred to as Layer 1 and 2 technology)
- 15% into DeFi projects (Decentralised Finance)
- 7% into the gaming / metaverse sector
- 7% into stable coins

Note that you can choose to hold multiple coins within one sector. For example, in DeFi where we allocate 15%, you may like to hold three coins with 5% allocated to each, or one coin with all 15% allocated. Just remember that the more coins you hold, the more time is involved in managing them.

Why do we diversify our capital in this way? Quite simply because it spreads the risk. We never want to be over-invested in any losers or under-invested in any winners.

Here is an example of a case study from the 2021 bull market applying the percent allocations above. I had hundreds of DWG members follow this portfolio and profit from it. You can see the percentage growth and how it turned relatively small amounts of money into life-changing wealth.

High Performing Growth Sector Portfolio
Case Study $20,000 [Bear to Bull]
Jan – Dec 2021

Project	Percent %	Amount $	Jan 2021 Price	Dec 2021 Price	Gain	Portfolio Now	
Bitcoin	32%	$6,400	$29,374	$46,306	57%	$10,048	Traditional/Conservative
Ethereum	18%	$3,600	$730	$3,714	409%	$18,324	
BNB	7%	$1,400	$38	$527	1287%	$19,418	
AVAX	7%	$1,400	0.65c	$91	13,900%	$194,600	New Blockchain Tech (Layer 1, 2)
Matic	7%	$1,400	0.018	$2.55	14,067%	$198,338	
DeFi (Coin 1: HEX)	7%	$1,400	0.013c	0.285c	2092%	$30,688	DeFi
DeFi (Coin 2: Aave)	7%	$1,400	$52.7	266	404%	$7,056	
Gaming (Coin 1: Enjin)	3.5%	$700	0.136c	$2.65	1849%	$13,643	Gaming / Metaverse
Gaming (Coin 2: PYR)	3.5%	$700	$2.1	$16	700%	$5,600	
USDC	7%	$1,400	$1	$1	Stable	$1,400	Stable Coins

Turning a $20,000 Investment Into $499,115 In 1 Year

Let's just pause for a moment and consider this: what other asset class could you invest in right now that would allow you to turn $20,000 into close to half a million dollars in one year?

It simply doesn't exist.

So, should you simply replicate the exact coins you see here? Not quite. There's another key factor that drastically impacts the performance of your portfolio. And that is cycles.

Look for First Cycle Gainers

When choosing coins in the growth sectors above, you want to include some allocation of cryptocurrencies that are yet to undergo their first major market cycle. Why do we look for these? Because the first cycle is when the best results in terms of gains can be achieved. Gains in the realm of 10x, 100x, even as high as 10,000x are very possible. Many DWG students and I can attest to this.

But here's where new investors get it wrong: they buy into cryptocurrencies that did extremely well on their *first cycle* and expect the same gains to occur. Historically, the first cycle is where we see the biggest price action, but they don't perform as well in subsequent cycles. So, use the above portfolio example as a guide, rather than a copy and paste of the exact coins. Focus on how the portfolio has been diversified across high performing growth sectors and look for newer coins in those sectors that you can substitute in that are yet to go through their first cycle.

Another way to understand first cycle gainers is to consider how many people are invested into a particular crypto coin or project. The larger the investor pool, the 'heavier' that crypto becomes, and the more drive and energy it needs to rise in value in the next cycle. Bitcoin is a perfect example of this.

In some cases, the newer the crypto, the fewer investors it has, the more parabolic its price movements can be.

So, when choosing cryptocurrencies, check how many cycles your chosen crypto has gone through and aim for new coins and projects that have just launched and are yet to go through their first cycle. As I've said many times, you want to be placing maximum upside potential in front of you.

Chapter 20

Frustration Breeds Opportunities

Frustration = Innovation
Innovation = Opportunity

When looking at any major advancement in our world, we have to remember that nothing starts as it ends, and nothing starts out perfectly.

If we cast our minds back to the introduction of the computer, did it launch on day one looking like the sleek computers and laptops we see today? No, it looked very different. But investors who understood the frustrations of that era knew that it was only a matter of time before those issues were solved.

And did all the opportunities in the dotcom boom arrive on day one? No, in fact, some of the best financial opportunities of that time came much later when the infrastructure could support it. It was investors who knew it was coming and positioned themselves accordingly that had the best success.

Which brings us to cryptocurrencies.

Right now, crypto is technically in its infancy—it's a little clunky, a little technical in nature and hasn't been streamlined to its final evolution. But as better infrastructure rolls out, I have no doubt we'll witness an increase of global adoption on both a retail and institutional level. Remember, it's the frustration within an ecosystem that spawns the best opportunities for investors and the best growth for the entire asset class. We just need to look for where the innovation is coming from and invest there, in my opinion.

Chapter 21

Make Your Portfolio Work for You

Staking is like having a license to print money.

Now that you've learned how to build your portfolio, let's take it a step further by scaling it through staking.

Staking is the process of locking up your crypto for a certain amount of time in order to earn more crypto as a reward. So, rather than simply buying and holding, you can generate additional, free crypto and turn your holdings into a dynamic, yield-generating machine.

This is game changing!

Staking works in a similar way to term deposit accounts at traditional banks, but the interest rates are significantly more alluring. They can range anywhere from 3% to 300%, allowing you to multiply your holdings and even generate an additional income. Think of it like a long-term savings strategy that delays gratification and supports a positive investment style.

Here's an example of one of my own staking experiences:

During the 2021 bull market, I was staking a crypto called ICOSA. I locked up 6,400 tokens, which at the time was worth $6,700 AUD.

After 180 days, I had generated 9,896 ICOSA tokens which were valued at $10,983 AUD. I'd actually earned more in interest than the principal amount I had staked. But here's the cherry on top—the crypto I was staking was appreciating in value while staked, in accordance with the market conditions.

This was just one staking opportunity of many that were available during that time, allowing me to grow my portfolio, earn yield upon yield and compound my earnings many times over. I was making anywhere from $1,000 USD to one Ethereum per day in collective income from my stakes (at the time, Ethereum was valued around $4,000 USD per coin). This is why I consider staking one of the most powerful tools to transform crypto holdings into dynamic, productive assets. In other words, a cash generating machine!

"A smaller but more consistent income stream earned through staking will often beat the occasional larger win earned through trading."
Coach Alex, Digital Wealth Group

Many investors think the way to scale their portfolio is to keep adding funds to their already growing account. But you can actually take the crypto you earn from staking and repurpose it within your portfolio. This means you're earning money for free (from the initial stake), which you reinvest to earn more money for free (from the next stake you put in place). And if you can do that, could you also get to a place in your investment timeline where you never add a single dollar of fresh capital again.

Yes, this is all very possible. This is the power of staking and long-term wealth creation. It's a compounding effect that takes time, but when done correctly, can drastically scale your portfolio and wealth. Like everything in crypto, staking gives you options. There is no pressure to stake. You can keep your assets liquid and still make incredible gains by using the strategies we've discussed so far. But if you want to take it to the next level, staking is a great way to do it.

We can either hold crypto and watch our portfolio fluctuate in the market. Or we can put our crypto to work and transform our portfolio into a productive asset as well.

Here are some things to know about staking:

1. **Yield appreciates:** The yield you earn on your stakes is pegged to the market price. This means if your staked crypto is going up in value, so is your yield.

2. **Yields are subject to market cycles:** When setting up a stake, you want to consider minimum stake lengths and market cycles. When you stake during a bear market, you could expect the yield earned to be a fraction of what you could potentially earn during a bull market. Setting up your stakes to start in a bear and become liquid in a bull is ideal. While it's impossible to time the exact moment of a bull market, we can use what we know about market timing to make an educated guess.

3. **You can gain exposure to different coins:** When you stake a coin, you sometimes have the option of earning the yield from that stake in another coin altogether. For example, you stake crypto coin A, and earn the yield in crypto coin B. This is a way to get exposure to an asset (crypto coin B) for zero investment. You can then either hold crypto coin B, swap it for another crypto coin, or cash it out at your discretion.

4. Different chains = different yields: Many people stake their crypto using apps that run predominantly on the Ethereum blockchain, but there are early staking opportunities on other blockchains that can produce even higher yield than what you're getting on Ethereum. It pays to look around.

Will You Be Defensive or Aggressive?

In order to turn the yield generated from staking into an additional income, you'll need to have a plan around what kind of staker you will be—defensive or aggressive.

If you're a defensive staker, you typically convert your yield into fiat currency and lock away the value the stake has created for you.

If you're an aggressive staker, you typically reinvest that yield and compound without withdrawing it.

You can also apply both strategies at once, depending on the type of stakes you have. So, if you're staking a crypto that pays the yield in a speculative coin, you may be more inclined to cash that out as there is an associated price volatility attached to that coin. But if you're earning yield in a conservative and safe crypto like Ethereum, it may make more sense to compound and earn more because of the long-term value and price appreciation we would expect from Ethereum.

Stakes Are Like Businesses

I like to think of stakes as a collection of small businesses, with each one generating cash flow that can be collected at different times. Some stakes require a lot of management and oversight, while some require very little, so this needs to be taken into consideration when building your staking ladder.

For example, your staking ladder could look like this:

- **Thirty Days** – Crypto A will finish its set staking period and produce around $1,000 USD. You can then re-stake for an additional thirty days.
- **Sixty Days** – Crypto A has finished its second staking period and generated another $1,000 USD. You can then re-stake for one-hundred days to slot in perfectly with the remainder of your ladder.
- **Ninety Days** – Crypto B will finish and this will generate approximately three ETHs.

Staking amounts listed in the above example are arbitrary numbers. Outcomes from your stakes will always depend on your investment total, stake length and varying other factors.

And the staking ladder continues to roll over in this fashion:

- **270 Days**
- **One Year**
- **Two Years**
- **Five Years**
- **Ten Years**
- **Fifteen Years**

As each stake ends, the interest earned from the locked crypto becomes liquid and you can sell it or re-stake (compound) it and place it strategically back in the ladder.

Word of warning: as your staking ladder evolves, it will require more time and effort. I suggest having a calendar with reminders and alerts in place so you don't miss an important staking deadline.

To summarise, staking is an incredible opportunity to maximise your earnings and participate in the networks you support while growing your portfolio at the same time. As always, navigate this space wisely, educate yourself and know the risks prior to staking.

Chapter 22

The Biggest Mistakes New Crypto Investors Make

The loudest noise and the shiniest objects in crypto are often designed to scam you out of your money. It's best to turn the noise off completely.

As we conclude Part 3 and before we move onto Part 4, I'd like to address the biggest mistakes investors make when entering this market for the first time. I share these to arm you with knowledge and ensure you don't make any potentially costly mistakes! It's a harsh but unfortunate truth that many platforms, services and apps are designed to *take* your money, not *make* you money. They play on human psychology and target unassuming investors, but they can be avoided by following the methods I've shared throughout this book.

Crypto is a safe and exciting asset class when done correctly. Avoiding these simple mistakes will have you miles ahead and secure in the knowledge that your assets are safe.

Turn Off the News

For many, the news is considered a reliable account of worldwide events. It's been a staple in our daily routines for years and has shaped many of our perceptions and beliefs. We may have grown up assuming the news was truthful and accurate, but it's become increasingly evident this is not always the case anymore. In reality, the news prioritises viewer engagement and uses carefully curated content to achieve it. The focus is not always now about objective truth, but often reflecting popular narratives, or pushing new ones.

When it comes to cryptocurrencies in the news, it's more about tapping into public sentiment and attracting viewers than delivering well-researched insights from legitimate crypto experts. They follow a script to gain viewers. They have done it many times before.

So, if you ever see the news teaching you how to buy a certain crypto coin, tread with caution. The news is often not an authority in this space, so take everything they say with a grain of salt. Be sceptical, be a contrarian, and use your education about market sentiment and timing as your true guiding compass.

Never Chase a Pump

If you see a crypto coin pumping in value, and fast, avoid the temptation to jump on it immediately. Coins that go viral and surge rapidly in price have been known to dump just as fast as they rise. Once it's out of the gate, be very mindful of chasing it because these sudden spikes are unpredictable. You may assume the price will continue to climb, but it often ends up plummeting and taking any profit you plan to make with it.

The truth about pumps is you never actually know who is behind them. Some happen quite organically, but others are manufactured and fuelled by social media groups. There are dedicated pump-and-dump schemes that use social media to announce their intentions to pump a certain coin and dump it at a pre-planned time. An unassuming investor who doesn't know about this unscrupulous behaviour can fall into a trap. They jump in, only to find the price dumps and all the liquidity is pulled out.

So, if you see a pump accompanied by overflowing social media sentiment, it's best to avoid it.

Ignore Hourly Price Changes

This lesson goes hand in hand with removing ourselves from the noise of the crypto market and focusing on the bigger picture. We do this to stay level-headed and not become driven by our emotions.

If you fixate on the hourly price action of many crypto charts, you'll often see wild fluctuations within short timeframes. These can create a sense of urgency followed by impulsive decisions you may live to regret. Social media platforms will pander to these extremes, so that in the space of a day you can see a collection of headlines that are diametrically opposed! It may look like they're providing overall market commentary, but in actual fact, it's all zoomed in to the micro activity and designed to get views only—at the detriment of the unassuming new investor.

Rather than focusing on hourly price charts, zoom out to see the big picture at play. It will lead to a much more stable crypto journey.

Don't Over Invest

The best way to manage your portfolio is to be emotionally detached from it. Investing an amount that is comfortable for you is a much better strategy than impulsively 'betting the house' so to speak. Remember to ask yourself: *'How would I feel if the market did a 90% correction?'* If the thought fills you with dread, you're investing too much.

Also, don't forget about DCA. You can always accumulate larger chunks when the markets drop, but DCA is a great way to steadily add to your portfolio without the emotional ups and downs.

Avoid Celebrity Noise

If you see a celebrity or well-known figure endorsing crypto, proceed with caution because this is a telltale sign of what's referred to as 'crypto shilling'. This is where a person of influence creates buzz around a coin by endorsing it, causing demand to rise and prices to pump. The celebrity gets paid, then the price tanks.

If you see this type of activity, look at the credentials of the person doing the endorsing. If celebrities or influencers who've shown no previous interest in crypto are suddenly flying the flag (and offering zero transparency about why), they are probably being paid to lure you into a bad investment. Some celebrities don't even realise this is happening. They trust the promotion like they would any other and have no idea that it's probably a scam. And what happens to the unassuming investors who fall for it? They get caught up in what we refer to as a rug pool.

Take every celebrity endorsement with caution, even the ones you would normally trust. If a crypto coin has good utility, good technology and can sustain itself, it will stand on its own merit without the endorsement of a celebrity.

Be Mindful of Fake Gurus

The emergence of fake gurus, crypto fund managers and self-proclaimed experts in crypto has become an alarming trend. They present themselves as seasoned professionals, but their credentials and experience are questionable at best. They rely on exploiting trust for their own gains. Again, we come back to trust.

Remember, the crypto market is relatively new, so doesn't yet have the same stringent regulation and oversight as traditional finance. This makes it fertile ground for people with ulterior motives to thrive unchecked.

Case in point: a famous influencer in 2017 had over 41,000 followers. He claimed to be a crypto expert, but if you dug a little deeper his history was there for all to see. He was a plastic surgeon, a wedding planner, a caterer and ran a printing service. Does this sound like someone who has the time to build deep crypto knowledge? That's why you always dig a little deeper into anyone who is a self-proclaimed guru.

Understand Your FOMO Level (Fear of Missing Out)

Your best investments will often feel the worst and the worst will often feel like your best.

This saying reminds us that the more euphoria there is around a coin or project, the more wary we should be of what we're investing into. FOMO can often replace logic with emotions, and we want to avoid that at all costs.

If you're feeling intense FOMO creeping in, let it be a signal to pause and conduct a self-check. Ask yourself: *'Am I making the best decision right now, or am I letting emotions take control?'*

Recognising and managing FOMO is essential for making sound investment decisions. We want to hone our ability to separate emotions from rational judgment, rather than letting the FOMO master us. It can mean the difference between success or failure in the next bull market.

If It's Too Good to Be True, It Usually Is

Scams are plentiful in the crypto space, particularly those that guarantee huge profits with minimal effort. They typically involve third party lending platforms or crypto trading bots that promise to multiply your initial investment and do all the work for you. These platforms take your money and show you a dashboard with impressive gains, but when you attempt to access them, you're met with a demand for a fee to unlock your funds. Once the fee is paid, the platform mysteriously shuts down, and your hard-earned money vanishes into thin air.

The common thread among these fraudulent platforms is their reliance on third parties—another company in between you and your crypto assets. This directly violates the number one rule of crypto safety—always have your funds in a wallet you control, where you own the private keys. Anything other than this is a risk.

Always remember, the safest way to create true wealth in this market, wealth that can be handed down for generations to come, is to have private custody of your crypto.

Can You See Themes?

You'll notice there is one common thread binding all these mistakes together—they all prey on human emotions. Whether it's third parties trying to manipulate our feelings, or services offered where the custody should rightfully be ours, these platforms entice us with the promise of huge gains, but there's a scam-like component hidden within. This is what I refer to as 'noise' in the crypto realm—misleading elements to distract us from our path.

But here's the truth: *crypto is very simple when we turn off the noise.*

The real essence of crypto cannot be taken away. It's about you, in complete control of your money. You educate yourself, capitalise on market timing, diversify into growth sectors and play the long game. This is the key to crypto investing and keeping your wealth safe, not just through the volatility, but through all the crypto noise, too. This noise will only get louder, but as long as we stay on course, we can safely and successfully navigate future market cycles.

Chapter 23

Are You Ready?

It is the ones that do crypto right.

I hope you've enjoyed this venture into portfolio building and making your crypto work for you. We've explored the ins and outs of keeping your digital assets safe, delved into crypto growth sectors and why they should be part of your portfolio, discussed the top mistakes new investors make and learned all about staking and passive income strategies. It's been an educational and insightful journey, and it's about to get even more exciting. Why? Because we're venturing into the realm of selling!

Everything we've learned so far is about positioning ourselves for this moment. The moment we sell and take profits. As we head off on this path, remember, this is a realm where the future is yours to shape.

This crypto journey is not just about owning coins, it's about learning how to sell them at the right time in the market.

PART FOUR

Take Profit And Unlock Financial Freedom

In my time as an educator, leading thousands of new investors on this path, I can safely say I've seen it all. I've witnessed success stories from people who armed themselves with knowledge, and I've seen missteps as investors charge in with high emotions that run the show. How do you ensure you're the first one and not the second? It all comes down to *education and emotional management*—particularly around selling.

In this section, I'll share some of my key strategies and insights around taking profit and creating the lifestyle of your dreams. This is about crafting your legacy and securing wealth that transcends generations. When you combine this section with the strategies shared earlier in this book, you'll not only see how enjoyable and rewarding this experience can be, but you'll also lay the groundwork for a portfolio that generates wealth and extra income streams for years to come.

The truth is, selling plays a pivotal role in your investment journey, but it's often one of the most overlooked aspects of crypto investing. Many people focus on the big gains from the next 100x coin, forgetting the transformative step in between! Selling is *the* crucial component that will convert your investments into tangible dreams. Becoming comfortable with the art of selling will not only set you apart from many thousands of investors out there, it will unlock the full power and potential of this asset class.

Let's dive in.

Let's Hear from Our Students

Lawrence, 57
Brisbane, Australia

"I started purchasing crypto in 2020, after ignoring my friend Max, who had been telling me about it constantly since 2013. I was never that interested before then, but when I saw that large institutions such as PayPal and Tesla were starting to buy crypto, I thought I should investigate.

I started by investing a substantial amount, $192,308.49, between 31 August 2020 to 31 August 2021. When that amount doubled, I then committed $1,977,985 AUD to a crypto project. This investment has grown significantly and is now worth $5,071,737.06, effectively increasing by five times. Remarkably, the initial investment has seen an impressive growth of forty-five times in value.

I am very glad I made the decision to invest in my own education in the crypto space. Having weekly one-hour coaching calls for a whole year, and continuing with monthly coaching thereafter, has been invaluable. This space changes rapidly, and knowledge is the key to success. The investment has paid for itself many times over. Looking back, of all the investment courses I have taken in my lifetime (share trading, option trading, property renovation, property development, running an eBay business), this is the only one that has been worthwhile and it has generated the greatest return. This knowledge has helped me identify projects that would perform well long term over many cycles in the future.

Without proper guidance, I know I would have lost all my funds in crypto with the collapse of various platforms and the rest of my funds in scam coins or trading. Also, I would have missed out on many early access opportunities to good new projects. I would not know how to earn yield safely without risking the portfolio with staking and mining. I'm happy to say that my passive income from mining, staking, and liquidity farming now exceeds my active income from business and other investments many times over.

As a result of this learning and understanding of this class of investment, I have confidently allocated most of my investment portfolio to this space. Crypto now accounts for 52% of my investment portfolio, and even in the current bear market, my portfolio is still up from the amount invested, thanks to the application of the knowledge I've acquired.

Coming from traditional finance (business and property investing), I understand how to leverage yield and borrowing to accelerate the growth of one's net worth using loans to enjoy gains without selling assets and incurring taxes. DeFi loans in crypto now allow me to do the same by borrowing against my crypto holdings (paying no interest) to help my children with the deposits required to buy their first homes and perhaps assist them in their future business ventures (medical centres). This is ultimately a benefit of successful crypto investing. Furthermore, I am now able to educate my family members and friends to also benefit from this emerging class of investment. It is definitely the highest performing investment, but only when approached correctly with the right knowledge.

Beyond the financial gains, my crypto success has enabled me to achieve meaningful life goals. I've had the privilege of inspiring my two daughters to start saving and investing for their future. As they progress in their careers, I look forward to fulfilling my promise of securing their financial future.

I am forever grateful to Sydel and the team for creating this leading learning platform for crypto. A big thank you to my experts for their guidance."

Chapter 24

A Lesson in History

*Have a plan when you're not emotional,
so that you have a plan when you are.*

In January 2018, the entire crypto market reached a staggering total market cap of $828 billion USD. This was contextually huge relative to previous cycles, and many people had turned small investments into hundreds of thousands of dollars, even millions! The excitement of watching those portfolio numbers skyrocket was palpable. In fact, I recall a friend showing me his portfolio tracker at the time and it was a rollercoaster of fluctuations. We watched it go from $1.6 million to $1.5 million to $1.7 million all in one night.

But here's where it gets interesting. Like many new crypto investors during these peak bull market times, my friend watched the numbers moving around, yet did nothing about it. And after the crypto all-time highs in January 2018, the market began to correct, and the downward journey started. Because as we know, this is what super cycles do.

In 2018, we saw the crypto market capitalisation bottom out at $101 billion USD, from its all-time high of $828 billion USD. That's an 84% drop across the entire market.

And my friend? He rode his profits back down to his initial investment without taking a dime.

This is a typical example of what happens during the peak of a bull market, where gains from astronomical highs gradually dwindle down 80-90%. In fact, very few people at that time took profits along the way. And if you remember our discussion in Part 2 about human emotions, in the Wall Street Cheat Sheet, this is known as the descent from euphoria to despair.

The lesson here is simple: life-changing gains are only life changing if we learn to sell.

You see, many new investors fall into the trap of thinking the number on their portfolio tracker is the number in their bank account, but that's not quite accurate. Yes, that is what your portfolio is worth, but it means nothing unless you can be disciplined enough to take profits and not let greed for higher prices take you over.

> "Profits on paper don't belong to you. They belong to the market."
>
> **Coach Michael, Digital Wealth Group**

So, my tip. Have a plan when you are not emotional, so that you have a plan when you are.

That friend I mentioned earlier? He was sitting on gains of over 2,500%. But instead of taking profit, he assumed the market would continue to rally. He listened to mass media and the price predictions of the crowd, and he believed every word. The lesson: sometimes you need to turn off the noise and look at things with some perspective. There's no other asset class where we'd be sitting on that much profit and not take some off the top. By following these cycles and procedures, you can begin to compound profits over many super cycles to come.

Chapter 25

Profit Taking Is Vision Creating

Your master vision lays on the other side of the sell button.

So, we've chosen our coins. We've entered the market at the right time. We've positioned ourselves for maximum upside and we're currently sitting on great gains. What comes next? Profit taking!

As I mentioned earlier, the amount you see on your portfolio tracking app is the figure the market *owes you. It is not the money in your bank.* You need to learn to take profit safely in order to collect. But what new investors learn very quickly is that taking profit is actually one of the hardest stages of the crypto journey. And it all comes down to one thing: emotions.

> "Buying is easy, selling (correctly) is difficult."
> **Coach Michael, Digital Wealth Group**

If you think learning about crypto and getting your head around the lingo and technology is challenging, try taking profits when you're sitting on 100x gains and you're second-guessing whether they will go up more. I've been in this situation many times and I can tell you it's one of the most anxious moments of the journey. Your emotions take over. You begin overthinking your exit timing and questioning whether you should be withdrawing now, or waiting another day (then another, then another).

This cycle will go on forever if you let it.

What helped me was connecting with this fundamental truth:

> ***There is no other situation where you would make 100x on your money and not take profits.***

To demonstrate this, let's compare the crypto market to the traditional investing scene. In traditional markets, a return of 10-20% from an actively managed, award-winning fund is seen as extraordinary. So many investors would have no problem withdrawing from it, yet in crypto, investors regularly sit on 1,000-5,000% gains and take no profit. Instead, they sit glued to the portfolio tracker and watch the gains slip through their fingers. Why? Because they let their emotions take over.

Greed starts calling all the shots.

So how do we counteract this? By having a strategy and a plan for profit taking. I recommend you take the time to think about what your personal goals for profit are. Will you withdraw a portion of your funds when your crypto does a 5x, a 10x, a 100x? Is there a particular figure you'd like to see each crypto reach? Think about this well before the bull market, because it will act as your anchor when the storm of euphoria hits. Investing in a disruptive and highly lucrative asset class is one thing, but protecting and securing that wealth and knowing how to take profits is quite another.

Does this mean you should take profits every time you make 5% or 10%? Not necessarily, but if you're sitting on 300% to 3,000% gains, then you should consider taking some cream off the top. Especially if the gains were generated in a short period of time.

> *"When it comes to buying and selling, the harder it is to push the button, the better your timing."*
> **Coach Gary, Digital Wealth Group**

Remember, nothing climbs upwards forever. Bitcoin's super cycles will happen again, because that's how markets work. We see the same major boom and bust trajectory in real estate, commodities, stocks and bonds. The difference with crypto is it can happen a lot faster, which is why I always remind people to know a profit when you see one.

Chapter 26

No One Has a Perfect Sell Record

"The key is to come away with a successful bull market engagement."

Coach Michael, Digital Wealth Group

When it comes to selling, many investors become fixated on the perfect time to take profit. But I encourage you, right now, to take that pressure off and remove any expectations of perfect timing. Why? Because it's rare to find an investor who consistently sells at the peak of the market. Even the experienced pros don't get it right all the time.

"You will make mistakes, place bad bets, mis-time the market. Regret is unavoidable. You just need to accept it and learn to manage it."

Coach Alex, Digital Wealth Group

The truth is experienced investors have a better understanding of markets and a firmer grasp of their own emotions. They know that wins *and* losses are part of every crypto journey, and you just have to take them as they come. I can tell you from my own experience that trying to time the market perfectly is a recipe for disaster.

So rather than chase perfection, I encourage you to aim for an educated guess, based on what you now know about market cycles. Adopt an attitude of entering and exiting at *approximately* the right time in the cycle. This will allow you to get close, without the stress that comes from attempting to time the top.

And once you've made the commitment to sell, be okay with your choice and avoid looking back on the price performance that followed the day you sold. While it feels great to know you timed it well, you can also find yourself disheartened to see that it doubled in value a month later. This is the volatility of the crypto market and it's simply the nature of the beast. Rather than beat yourself up, congratulate yourself on having made the move. After all, this is what we're all in this game for. Sure, other investors may have held onto their crypto for longer, but that doesn't mean they fared any better than you. You could have potentially reaped more of the reward simply by taking the profit when it was there.

When it comes to selling, nothing is etched in stone and there is no right or wrong way to do it. It's about what makes sense to you and what aligns with *your* master vision. So, when you're looking to take profit, embrace the mindset of 'I've made money and I'm going to enjoy withdrawing it', rather than 'I have to time the market perfectly or else I've failed'.

Next, let's get into some top selling strategies.

Chapter 27

Selling Strategies and Concepts

"Don't get emotionally attached to your cryptos."
Coach Gary, Digital Wealth Group

We've now come to one of the most exciting phases in a new investor's crypto journey, which is also one of the most challenging. Why? Because intangible factors come into play when it's time to sell:

1. The uncertainty of the market. Investors grapple with the imminent threat of pullbacks and find themselves in a constant guessing game about when to sell.
2. FOMO. Investors have regrets about when they chose to sell and tell themselves they could have achieved more.

The struggle with these two things is very real.

As discussed earlier, on the way to the top of a super cycle, it's normal for the market to pull back a number of times, and 10-30% pullbacks are commonly seen. So, an investment of $100,000 could drop to $70,000. For the emotional or unaware investor, this could trigger a flurry of thoughts such as 'this could be the end' or 'I wish I'd taken more profit when my portfolio was worth $100,000'.

However, just like that, and within weeks (even days), the market re-corrects, and prices jump higher than ever before, leading new investors to have a restored confidence and falsely believe that *'this bull market is never going to end'*. Until it does.

Why is this important to know? Because any investor who doesn't plan for this will find themselves completely untethered while riding the emotional rollercoaster of a bull market. It may be exhilarating, but as we've discussed previously, emotions do not make for a savvy investor. Having a strategy and some education around the skill of selling will set you miles ahead of the crowd.

While there's no right or wrong way to take profits, there are some important things you should take into consideration.

1. What Is Your Plan with The Profit?

Many new investors think selling crypto means cashing out and depositing the funds straight into a bank account. While this is one option, there are also a few more you may like to think about:

> **The Conservative Swap:** This involves swapping a speculative (higher-risk) crypto for a lower-risk crypto like Bitcoin or Ethereum. This will increase your allocation in conservative and lower-risk assets, which could appeal to some crypto investors.
>
> **The Speculative Swap:** Another option is to rotate part or all of the profit from one crypto into another that is more speculative. The benefit being that speculative, higher risk coins, particularly those on their first cycle, can have the potential of parabolic gains.

The Stable Coin Swap: Lastly, you may like to consider taking your profit and converting it into a stable coin, which is the closest thing to holding crypto cash you can get. Stable coins act like dry powder in your portfolio, meaning you have capital sitting there in the form of an exchangeable stable coin.

"If you are holding an old coin in your portfolio because you want it to get back to break even, ask yourself 'would I buy that coin now?' If the answer is 'no' then consider selling it and rotating to another opportunity."

Coach Michael, Digital Wealth Group

These are just some of the options to consider as you formulate your own plans for each of the cryptos you hold and the direction you want to take them. You may not know what that looks like now, but it's good to understand the options available to you.

2. Signals and Triggers for Selling:

When we sell, we want to sell in chunks, rather than removing our entire positions all at once. Below are some of my favourite beginner-friendly ways to take profit while keeping your portfolio working for you.

The Free Ride: A conservative approach to selling is to withdraw your initial investment when your portfolio doubles. This means you're playing with nothing but profit, and you are now in it for the free ride. In other words, all your risk has been removed and all future gains are from growing only profit.

The Bragging Indicator: If you find yourself showing off your gains or even just taking a moment yourself to admire the multiple figures on your screen, it's time to consider taking profit. We experience these moments at various stages of the bull market, so when it comes around again (and it will) profit-taking is most likely a smart choice. If you're refreshing your tracking app ten times a day, let that be a signal to yourself to consider withdrawing anywhere from between 5-10% of your portfolio profits. You'll be grateful you did.

Zoom Out, Get Perspective: When you're in the middle of a bull market and emotions are high, it's common to want to hold out for that one extra pump that you hope will come. But you need to also consider the bigger picture by comparing the bear market to the bull market. You may be looking for an extra 50-100% price increase out of your crypto, but how much has it already climbed relative to the bear market low? You could already be looking at a figure that has climbed 1,000-3,000% from the bottom! This is why it's essential to have a balanced view and understand the gains you're sitting on. It's not just about the percentage. You need to look at the context behind those numbers and how much it may have already moved.

3. Dollar Cost Averaging Out of The Market

I've talked about DCA as a powerful tool for investing into crypto without emotions. Now what if I told you that same strategy can be used to exit out of the market as well. I call it reverse-engineered

DCA and it's a smart, low-risk way to sell your crypto. Think of it as a smooth ride out of the market. Because unless you're a trader or have a crystal ball, exiting your crypto positions can feel like taking a wild guess. Reverse-engineered DCA is the solution to this guessing game.

When I Turned $1,000 into $108,790 in Ninety Days

In 2017, I invested in a crypto called NEO. It was worth 0.44c at the time and I purchased $1,000 worth. Within a period of ninety days, NEO was up over 10,879% and my $1,000 was now sitting at $108,790. I decided to cash out the entire position for a large sum of Bitcoin at the time. Had I applied dollar cost averaging though, I would have held my position longer and experienced NEO's second wave, which would have seen my $1,000 turn into almost half a million. Either way, it was still a great win.

The Lesson

Don't remove the entire position at once, but rather use DCA to gradually take profit along the way.

4. Practice Selling:

It's wise to have a plan for selling your crypto, but it's even better to know how to execute it. That's why I always recommend you practice selling with a small amount of crypto first.

> *"About to sell a significant amount of crypto? Always sell a test transaction first!"*
>
> **Coach Alex, Digital Wealth Group**

Implementing a test run with a small transaction isn't just about knowing which buttons to click, it's about helping you identify and manage the emotions that arise during a sale—be it excitement, anxiety or even fear. It's better to navigate these feelings with a smaller amount before handling larger sums.

5. Tax, Tax and More Tax

Tax is often overlooked when thinking about selling, but it's an inevitable part of the crypto journey, so being prepared and asking the right questions early can help minimise your tax debt later. Every country has different tax laws and regulations, but there are similar themes from major economies worth noting. It's wise to team up with a crypto-savvy accountant who can double check the tax laws of your country. The more questions you ask, the clearer your understanding of your tax implications becomes.

Many new investors think a taxable event only occurs when you cash out crypto and put the fiat currency into your bank account. But a taxable event also occurs in many jurisdictions when you trade one cryptocurrency for another. So, if you sell Crypto A to buy Crypto B, you've technically created a taxable event. This is what's known as crystallising profits.

When we factor in the volatility of the crypto market, however, there's another layer of complexity. Let's work through an example.

Say you sell Crypto A for $10,000. In some jurisdictions, the moment you clicked 'sell' you raised a taxable event, regardless of what you did with it afterwards. So, let's say the tax from the sale of Crypto A came to $3,000.

Now, let's say you take that $10,000 from Crypto A and roll it into Crypto B. But unfortunately, Crypto B drops in value by 50% and now it's only worth $5,000. Now you have a bigger issue on your hands because, unless you sell Crypto B for $5,000 and crystallise the loss, you technically cannot claim that loss against the tax you have to pay from the sale of Crypto A.

Do you see how it just became a tricky situation? This is why you should understand the tax implications of your country when you're planning to sell.

Now let's move onto the tax implications for staking.

In some jurisdictions, staking is considered personal income. Therefore, if you generate $1,000 USD in yield, it's considered an extra $1,000 of income, regardless of whether you cashed it out or not. When the stake ends, and you un-stake that crypto, you've crystallised additional income in that moment.

I've seen investors deal with this in a number of ways.

1. Remove the staked income and cash it out into fiat currency.
2. Hold on to the yield, particularly if you're earning it in another cryptocurrency such as Ethereum. This is particularly smart during a bull market. Investors who do this understand that the value of that crypto can appreciate significantly, so

they are maximising their return. On the contrary, in other market conditions, if the income depreciates in value for whatever reason, you'll still pay tax at the rate calculated when you un-staked it.

As you can see, at this point in time, there's simply no avoiding tax in crypto. Some investors will go to great lengths to reduce their tax, even going as far as relocating to another country that recognises the economic value of crypto and offers lower taxation rates. In fact, there are countries that have created entire strategies to attract crypto millionaires and billionaires through extremely appealing tax rates.

It's a clever strategy if you ask me.

6. Liquidity Is Key

Ever wondered why a small investment in certain cryptocurrencies can cause their prices to skyrocket while the giants like Bitcoin and Ethereum seem unfazed? It's all about the size of the investor pool and the concept of liquidity.

I've talked about how liquidity plays a role in the exchange you choose. It's a crucial part of selling your crypto, particularly the more speculative coins. Remember, the impressive profit that you see on your portfolio tracker means nothing if there's not enough liquidity in that particular market for you to be able to sell what you want to. It's not so much of an issue with smaller amounts, but the larger the amount you want to buy or sell, the more of a role it will play. This is one of the largest misconceptions new investors face when going to take profit, and it was recently experienced by a DWG student.

Joahn Turns $900 into $9,000,000 in Three Months

Joahn, a student of DWG since 2021, invested into a new speculative asset we had brought to our students' attention. The coin went parabolic and his $900 turned into over $9 million in just three months. But when Joahn went to cash out his profits, he faced an issue—only three exchanges had enough liquidity to do the transaction. Joahn wanted to swap the coin into Ethereum (which he could then sell for fiat dollars). He managed to cash out by spreading the amount across three different exchanges, but he could only withdraw approximately $700,000 at a time due to the liquidity.

As you can see, this is an extraordinary profit and it was a great move for Joahn to have exposure to this coin. But it comes with a lesson: pay attention to liquidity.

So, how do these smaller crypto coins have such astronomical gains compared to the traditional giants like Bitcoin and Ethereum? It all comes down to market capitalisation.

If a coin or project has a market cap of only a few million, that means a few hundred thousand dollars entering into that coin can push the price up significantly. Whereas Bitcoin and Ethereum's price barely changes by a fraction of a dollar when a few hundred thousand dollars has been purchased. In fact, you can generally sell large amounts of these cryptos with just one click. Why? Because the investor pool is huge, with millions of investors globally, so it takes a massive wave of buyers or sellers (or one crypto whale) to move that price.

A rule of thumb for liquidity is the smaller the market cap (aka the more speculative the coin), the riskier it tends to be. However, it's also where profits can multiply the fastest.

Note: you can check the liquidity of any cryptocurrency by searching it on an aggregator website and clicking on 'Markets'.

Chapter 28

How Will You Sell?

Learning to sell correctly is how we bring our wealth vision to life.

Now you know some of the concepts and strategies you could use to sell, let's look at the logistics of moving your crypto back into fiat currency.

The crypto buying and selling cycle looks something like this:

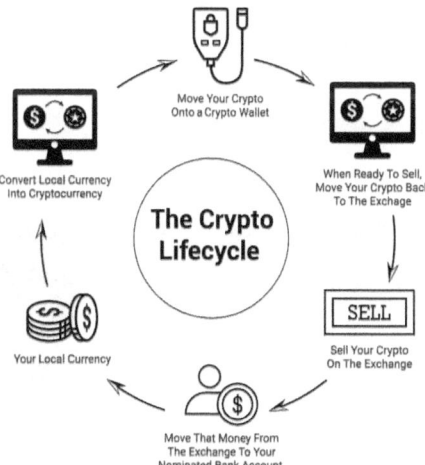

Depending on your bank, this entire process can happen in as little as one day. However, it's not uncommon for it to take a little longer the first time you sell. This is because the exchange may want to verify your ID and ensure you are who you say you are, and not a scammer.

Selling crypto is generally easy, and there are a few ways you can do it. The easiest exchanges have the highest fees, but as you become a more confident investor, you can explore lower fee options.

Let's break down the ways to sell:

1. Market Price

This is the simplest and most straightforward way to sell your crypto. You simply transfer your crypto from your hardware wallet back to the exchange, then hit the 'sell' button to sell it back to the exchange you bought it from. You'll be selling at the market price, which may not be the best possible price out there, but it's the quickest and easiest method. Once you've sold the crypto on the exchange, you can nominate a bank account to move your fiat currency straight into.

2. Limit Order

An alternative to selling at market is agreeing to sell your crypto when it reaches a predefined price. For example, if you want to buy Bitcoin, but you're happy to wait until it drops slightly, you can set a 'limit buy order' and specify the exact price at which you're willing to make that purchase. The order will not be filled until the Bitcoin price you've set has been reached. Investors use limit orders to buy lows when a capitulation event occurs in a bear market. We see this a lot with Bitcoin and Ethereum as I mentioned in the previous example.

You can also set limit orders to sell crypto at record prices during a bull market. As soon as the price transacts at the specified amount, the order will be filled. That Bitcoin is held on the exchange and ready to sell the moment the price is right, meaning it is no longer freely available in your portfolio. And if circumstances change and you need to make your crypto liquid and available once again, you can simply cancel the limit order.

I believe limit orders are a great way to transact if you can spare the time to wait out the moves of the market. You can get quite strategic with limit orders, placing them at different price points so you can enter or exit at favourable levels. There is also the added benefit of you not having to watch the price and manually click the buy or sell button.

3. Over the Counter (OTC)

OTC involves brokering a deal with an exchange to lock in a better rate than if you were to just click 'sell'. It's a private, convenient option because the transactions are off the public order book and offer good execution, speed, privacy and flexibility. It's great for selling substantial amounts because the money you save on fees can be in the thousands. You may even request a broker or private representative from the exchange to be your personal contact when you want to sell large amounts.

If you're in this position, I recommend that prior to selling, you reach out to two or three exchanges you're registered on and negotiate the best rate with a broker. They'll typically hold that rate for a set period of time, so you can select the best price and get the best exchange into fiat currency.

I hope you've enjoyed learning the different strategies and ideas for selling crypto. This is an important part of bringing your vision for wealth to life. Next, let's look at how you can take those profits and create the freedom you desire.

Chapter 29

Unlocking Freedom

Freedom is not just an idea. It's a belief system, a way of life, and a reality that crypto places within your reach.

When you get to the point in your crypto journey of taking profits and reaping rewards, all sorts of stories start to arise. I find this is an excellent opportunity to reconnect with one of the reasons we're all here—self-sovereignty and financial freedom.

From a very young age, we're conditioned into a certain way of thinking, with a degree of enslavement attached to our beliefs. We're told that success and freedom are something we must work hard for and dedicate years, even decades of our life to, but what if we were offered freedom for much less work? What if there was a way for us to make money that we have full control of, simply by capitalising on a ground-breaking financial system and applying what we know about market timing?

Would we believe it, even if it contradicts what we've been indoctrinated with?

Many people struggle with this concept. It's a revolution in thought that defies everything we've been told about financial security. The idea that we could achieve freedom through cryptocurrencies challenges so many of our deeply rooted beliefs, we don't allow ourselves to imagine it could be true. But crypto is one of those opportunities. It can do in two to four years what we've been told takes a whole lifetime to achieve. It's a door to freedom that can be opened by anyone.

Freedom is yours to take, life is yours to create, and crypto offers a faster and more accessible route to financial freedom than we've ever seen before.

What does freedom mean to you? What is your dream for your life? For some, it's the power to make choices without financial constraints. For others, it's the ability to live life completely on their own terms. For me, it's the ability to focus on my passions—the true freedom that comes from putting my knowledge into action now. Whatever it means for you, the essence of freedom is universal—it's about having the autonomy to shape your life just the way you want.

So many of us say we want freedom, but when offered the path to attain it, we become uncomfortable. Our mental walls have been reinforced so many times over the years that we simply can't imagine a way out of them. We've essentially constructed our own prisons to entrap us in false beliefs. While this isn't necessarily our fault, it is our responsibility to demolish the walls and set ourselves free.

Your success in crypto is a brand-new avenue that doesn't need to be linked to success or failure in other areas of your life. If I'm proof of anything, it's that your past never has to dictate your future and you can, at any point, redefine an exciting, abundant and incredible life for yourself.

So, are you ready to put yourself first and go the whole way to make this a reality? To experience an incredible and enriching life filled with great experiences and financial freedom? I'm talking about giving this your all, because you are worth going the *entire* way for.

So, I ask you, what kind of life do you want to create?

Let's Hear from Our Students

Rob and Tamara
Dawesville, Western Australia

"Through our journey in cryptocurrencies, we've achieved remarkable success with our crypto investments realising a remarkable 500% gain. This journey has been an opportunity to expand our knowledge about crypto and benefit from expert support, and the results have been truly gratifying."

Ruth, 76
Melbourne, Australia

"Since I started investing in cryptocurrencies in May 2020, I've seen almost a threefold increase in their value, which is truly amazing! What's even more exciting is that both of my children have also ventured into the world of cryptocurrencies, and they've earned significantly more than they would have through traditional banking or other investment options. I'm not only excited for my own crypto journey but also for the promising future ahead for my children in this space."

Martin, 47
Cairns, Australia

"Since delving into the world of cryptocurrency, my investments have experienced remarkable growth. In my first ever experience of selling, I made a 60% profit as I did not want to run the risk of losing my capital. Later, I put more money into crypto, turning $190,000 into $1 million so far."

PART FIVE

Elevate Your Mindset, Master Your Life

I trust you've enjoyed discovering more about cryptocurrencies, market cycles and how to construct a winning crypto portfolio. Now let's move onto perhaps the most important component in your wealth-building journey—mindset. I'm a passionate advocate for mindset work and I believe getting this right is absolutely crucial for investing in crypto. Why? Because we cannot have a $5 million portfolio with a $5,000 mindset.

In my years as an investor and educator, I can tell you that the cyclical nature of the crypto market will take every part of your mindset and amplify it. It will shine a spotlight onto all areas of your life, particularly your money beliefs. Nothing will supercharge your understanding of your mindset faster than the crypto market. This asset has produced enormous wealth for people at unprecedented speed, much faster than any other asset on the planet. However, fast wealth can lead to fast mistakes.

So, how do we adequately plan for wealth? How do we avoid Sudden Wealth Syndrome and begin the journey to self-mastery and a prosperous mindset? It starts with examining our thoughts, challenging our narratives and questioning the stories we tell ourselves about money.

In other words, it starts with applying a concept I call *radical self-evaluation*.

Within this section, I've included my top strategies for elevating your mindset, questioning your beliefs around money and aligning yourself with the wealth and prosperity that can come from this asset class. These methods are based on years of experience in my own journey as a crypto and mindset educator, and guiding thousands of investors since 2017 to achieve financial success. You'll find the most concise, poignant and relevant tips and tricks to fine tune your money mindset and position yourself for maximum success.

Let's begin.

Chapter 30

The Crypto Surprise

No one ever thinks this kind of wealth will happen for them, until it does.

I've seen it time and time again—new investors who set out on their crypto journey and underestimate the power of this asset class—drastically. They downplay the potential of crypto and assume the big gains could never happen to them. They often think small, but this is a mistake.

Crypto is not just another investment avenue. It's an absolute powerhouse in a league of its own. It may be hard to imagine what a 2x, a 10x or even a 100x potential gain feels like, but I can assure you it's entirely possible. Crypto has the ability to defy everyone's expectations and there's no other asset class that can match the dynamism and potential of this space.

But here's the thing: when new investors turn relatively small amounts of money into life-changing wealth and financial freedom, they come face to face with every single one of their money stories—the good and the bad. This is precisely why we want to shape our mindset in readiness for the success that lies ahead.

So, here's my suggestion: start now. Start to envision what a bright and abundant future might look and feel like. Start having positive conversations about it with the people you know and trust. But most of all, continue to educate yourself about the incredible asset class that is cryptocurrency. It's time to align yourself with your vision of financial freedom and reshape your relationship with money. Let's learn to dissolve the old money stories as they arise.

Chapter 31

What Are Your Stories?

*Taking control of your narrative is far more powerful than
leaving it to fate.
Let awareness be the compass that guides you through.*

We become weighed down by our stories in so many ways. We can be quite attached to them, to the point that we adopt them as our identity. But if we want to create true freedom, we need to bring conscious awareness to what we're carrying and recognise where it could be dragging us down. I'm talking about the deeply held, possibly unconscious beliefs that arise when we think about financial freedom.

Let's start with the most common stories I hear as a crypto educator:

- My family isn't wealthy, so how can I expect to be?
- I'm not smart enough to learn about crypto.
- I already have enough. To want more is greedy.
- I feel like an imposter. I don't belong here.
- Money is the root of all evil and I only need a little bit.
- How can I desire wealth when so many people are poor?
- I've always resented wealthy people. I'm not sure I want to be one.
- Money doesn't buy happiness.

- I have to work hard for every dollar. That's the way the world works.
- Debt is just part of life.

Do you know what most of these stories have in common? They're rooted in past experiences and conditioning. We've given them power by accepting them as truth, but it doesn't have to stay that way. These past stories are acting like invisible barriers, sabotaging our financial growth and potential.

So, what do we do? Well, we identify these thought patterns and consciously release them. But here's the trick: I'm not actually asking you to change, I am asking you to accept. This is the first step to releasing sabotaging patterns.

You see, many of us know we carry limiting beliefs, but we may not want to admit it or do the work to release them. This is where acceptance and awareness come in. When we have awareness, things simply cannot have the same control over us as they did before. It's about bringing the unconscious forward and being honest about the beliefs we carry, whether we like them or not. When we stop running from the preconceived perceptions of ourselves, we can accept ourselves as we truly are.

So, I invite you to deeply reflect on the stories you've been telling yourself about money and freedom. Perhaps even write them down so you can give them your full consideration. And remember, it's not about fixing, it's about bringing awareness and acceptance.

Chapter 32

How Do You Spend Your Time?

Crypto will continue to produce millionaires, whether you're onboard or not.

If you could walk through a door right now that gave you a shortcut to financial freedom, would you take it? Or would you put it off for another day? How much time would you devote to learning about something that could potentially change your life?

The reality is, cryptocurrencies have produced more millionaires, and at a faster rate, than any other asset on the planet. So, when I hear people say they'll focus on crypto another time or that they've turned their back to it for now, my response is always the same.

If you turn your back on crypto, the fastest appreciating asset in the world, what are you turning to instead?

In other words, if you truly and wholeheartedly desire financial freedom, why would you turn away from an asset that gives you the best chance of attaining it? If we're going to create a different way of living, with a fairer and freer and more sovereign world than we have now, we must take action in a different direction. So many of us go to work for forty, fifty, sixty hours each week to generate money. Yet, how many hours per week do we dedicate to creating financial freedom?

Our society has us programmed to believe that overworking ourselves is natural, but if you had financial freedom, would you still choose to spend forty, fifty, sixty hours each week working? Or would you choose pursuits that make you happy and fill you with purpose? If we removed the pressure of outstanding bills, how would you choose to spend your time?

Which brings me to my next question. How much time and energy do you spend each week creating a different future for yourself? Do you prioritise a daily grind with capped earning potential, or do you carve out time to focus on constructing an entirely new future?

If we keep doing the same thing without change, how can we possibly expect to achieve a different result?

I believe life is about recognising our choices and gaining mastery over our time. I no longer see crypto as just another thing competing for my time. I see it as the ultimate *giver* of time.

It's a small shift in perception, for a very big reward.

Chapter 33

Unpacking Your Aversion to Wealth

When we trap ourselves in scarcity, we deny ourselves an abundant and prosperous reality.

Now let's talk about one of the biggest reasons we're all here—creating wealth.

Money is seen as a symbol of power, success and influence in our world, but it can trigger complex emotions and beliefs. For some of us, there exists an underlying aversion to wealth because we associate it with capitalism and greed. While this is understandable, it's not doing us any favours. We're simply keeping ourselves trapped in a cycle of financial scarcity.

The reality is, money is the currency of our world. It provides the means to live life on our terms and contribute to the causes we believe in. So even if we've convinced ourselves otherwise, or have aversions to what it represents, financial success is the key to a remarkably different experience in this life. I personally believe this is one of the lessons we're here to master, along with personal relationships, fulfillment and good health. Once we've checked off the financial freedom box, we'll find that many other things drop effortlessly into place. We find a sense of liberation and can direct our time and energy towards things that make us happy—deeper connections, personal growth and contributing positively to the world around us.

How do we make the transition? Well, all too often I hear people defining themselves with limiting language that sabotages their financial potential. Literally making themselves poor. They've embraced a belief that settling for less is perfectly okay. While acceptance for a personal situation is admirable, it becomes detrimental when we're trying to build wealth, particularly if it's laced with a hidden judgment, subconscious fear or resistance to wealth.

A healthier perspective is one that allows for financial abundance without the guilt or negative connotations. We must open ourselves up to the possibility of receiving wealth and welcome it with open arms. It's about recognising that financial prosperity doesn't mean we have to change the essence of who we are. It can coexist with our desires, aspirations and personal values.

In my own journey, I found the wealthier I became, the easier my life became and also the more exciting because I was attracting new and unique experiences into my life. Without ever trying to, I found myself in circles with wealthy people where money worries were a thing of the past. But it was more than that, because the wealthier I became, the less stress I carried, which allowed me to live a life in alignment with my passion and purpose.

Financial freedom is more than just money in the bank. It is a way of life that I encourage you to create. When we build wealth, we also go on a journey of building confidence in ourselves, and crypto is one of the tools that opens those doorways. So, I encourage a shift towards an empowered relationship with wealth. Be conscious of limiting language around money—it's not something a lucky few can have, it's in abundance and can be welcomed into your life any time you choose.

Now, let's explore this further with some practical ways to get comfortable with wealth.

Chapter 34

Becoming At Ease with Wealth

When financial abundance and wealth are your norm, you begin to see the fallacy.
Struggle and suffering are the lie that we have been sold.

When I was in my twenties, I was exposed to many wealthy and abundant people. I'm talking millionaires, billionaires and people who bought Bitcoin when it was just cents in the dollar. And I noticed that every single one of them had something in common—they all had a natural ease around wealth and abundance. To them, financial freedom wasn't a dream, it was a fundamental truth. They were effortlessly and naturally convinced that abundance was their birthright. As I examined this more closely, I saw they'd all done one particular thing to cultivate this attitude and create their dream life.

They decided what their 'normal' was going to be.

You see, these people saw everything in life as an offer—one they were free to accept, reject or renegotiate as they saw fit. So, the standard model that most of us grew up with wasn't going to cut it for them. They chose another path entirely, one where wealth and abundance were not aspirations but normal expectations in life.

Let's just stop here for a moment...Why have we, as a society, agreed that financial freedom is a dream only a lucky few can have? Why do we see debt, mortgages, illness and never-ending stress as a normal way to exist? And why do we view people who don't live this way as so different?

What an inversion of truth.

From early childhood onwards, our cultural conditioning and social engineering model a certain way of life to us where structured curriculums replace natural joy, discovery and creativity. As we transition to the workforce, we learn that long hours and a conforming attitude are what pave the way for career advancement. Even in sports, we're taught to push ourselves beyond our limits to earn recognition. This framework operates within a flawed system, one that ensnares us in cycles of scarcity and relentless stress.

Put simply, it's a system that has people trapped.

Picture this instead: the freedom to work on projects that inspire you and those around you, without compromising your livelihood. The ability to add value to the world in alignment with your passions and purpose. The ability to support the communities you're a part of in ways that you choose. The time and energy to spend with your family, friends and loved ones. The feeling of being in alignment and energised rather than overworked and worn down. The peace that comes with never having to worry about bills or mortgages or rent ever again.

This is what I believe is normal.

So, I ask you, if we've been successfully programmed to have a certain view of life, where we all follow the same roadmap and we're all bound by varying limitations, could we program ourselves to have a limitless one?

The answer is yes. It cannot be true one way and not the other.

We absolutely can dismantle our old beliefs around money, wealth and freedom. We can conquer the illusion of lack and challenge the idea that only a few 'lucky' people can be financially free. We can make different choices in our thoughts, words and actions and we (and only we) can define what we'd like our normal to be.

Do you want to know the fastest way to do this? Surround yourself with wealth:
- Indulge in a luxurious fine dining experience.
- Browse in high-end designer stores.
- Test drive that dream luxury car.
- Register to inspect an exclusive house/apartment for sale.
- Surround yourself with people who are smarter and weather than yourself and talk openly about money and the possibility of financial freedom with those you can trust.

Each of these actions elevates you and helps you become comfortable in the vibration and energy of wealth.

Even if luxury shopping isn't your usual cup of tea, I encourage you to walk into a high-end store and hold their most extravagant item, or better yet, try it on!

What narratives emerge when you do this? This is about more than experiencing the luxury lifestyle for an hour or a day. It's about witnessing what comes up for you when you do. Rather than try to alter your behaviour, simply notice and accept yourself precisely as you are. The more you immerse yourself in the energy of abundance and affluence, the more you'll organically align yourself with any version of the future you desire.

Becoming at ease with wealth is one of the first steps to cracking through limiting beliefs and releasing trapped energy surrounding your own financial freedom.

Next, let's look at the other major factor when it comes to limiting beliefs—consent.

Chapter 35

We Live in a Consent-Based Realm

I have created everything.

It's an intimidating thought, isn't it ... the notion that we've created everything in our lives, from the homes we're living in, to the people around us, to the job we're doing and the food we eat? It all started with a thought that was followed up with an action, and it all stemmed from our consent. I truly believe we live in a consent-based realm, and despite appearances, we have a choice in everything we do, even when it seems that external forces are at play.

This belief is not just a philosophical idea, it's a tool for personal empowerment. When we see that choice is at the core of our existence, we go from being victims of circumstance into agents of change. This concept prompts us to take full responsibility for ourselves and our choices, something which is fundamental to investing in cryptocurrency. When we see that we have agency, we can move away from a mentality where 'life just happens to us' and into a more empowered stance of 'I create my life'.

The truth is, from the moment we open our eyes in the morning until we close them at night, we are either giving or withholding our consent. We're making micro-decisions all the time and with every choice, we're confirming what we'll accept in our lives—whether through active decisions or passive acquiescence.

What do I mean by acquiescence? Well, there are things we comply with that we haven't expressly consented to, but we go along with them anyway, often because we think we have no choice. It's a passive form of agreement or compliance, but it's still a choice we're making. I'm sure you'll find that even seemingly involuntary actions or difficult life moments have a choice embedded within them.

The concept of a consent-based realm can be triggering because it goes against everything we've been told about how the world works. But also, if everything is based on consent, that means the responsibility for everything in our lives rests completely with us. And many people just don't want to hear that.

But here's the thing: the more we think about this concept, the more intentional we are about what we give our consent to, the more empowered we become and the clearer it is that we are creating everything in our lives, including our financial situation.

So, what should we do once we become aware that everything revolves around our consent? We start to become more conscious of our decisions and actions. We begin to recognise that we have the ability to perpetuate a pattern or stop a situation dead in its tracks.

For example, I hear investors say they don't have enough time to devote to crypto education, or that life is too chaotic and busy for them right now. I truly believe that with every moment, we can invite a different outcome, different thought and different behaviour. It starts with awareness which eventually becomes a new way of being for ourselves.

If you don't have time to learn about crypto, create more time, even if it's just thirty minutes every second day.

If you're not computer-literate, start small and work big.

If you don't have confidence, create it by taking positive action.

Make choices and consent to a pathway that will lead you to the outcome you desire in your life, not what you think life is serving to you.

Chapter 36

Every Action in Crypto Places You a Step Ahead

Financial freedom is available for anyone who believes it will be a reality for them.
The human mind is quite unstoppable.

Crypto is an asset that is often misunderstood, and stepping into it requires you to swim against a tide of naysayers and sceptics. So many people are afraid of crypto and would rather wait for the comfort of mainstream acceptance before diving in. But as we know, they risk missing out on the monumental gains. As an educator in this space, I've seen both sides of the argument, and I've come to understand a profound truth about education: every single action you take in crypto is a step forward.

When you take the time to learn about crypto, you are placing yourself ahead of those who choose not to explore. Every piece of knowledge gets you closer to the life you want to build and the wealth you want to create. Crypto gives us an instant feedback loop where we don't need to spend years learning this asset class to see results. We can start learning and have success reflected back to us almost instantly. This inspires us to take further action and keep amassing these nuggets of educational wisdom.

I believe many of the pioneers who made millions in the early days of crypto once faced ridicule for their foresight. They embraced a technology ahead of its time, an asset class that was misunderstood. While we've moved past that pioneer stage, we are still early investors, and we still have the golden opportunity to shape our future like those early crypto adopters once did.

So, no matter how big your stride, every step you take in your crypto journey has meaning and merit. You are writing a new reality with every investment, with every piece of knowledge you acquire and every time you show up for yourself to create financial freedom. Whether you're spending thirty minutes each week or thirty hours, never underestimate the value of what you're doing. When you educate and invest in crypto, you are taking charge of your narrative, one step at a time.

Chapter 37

Don't Wait for Crypto to Grab You

Be proactive, not reactive.

From the euphoria of a bull market to the chill of a gruelling crypto winter, if there's one thing that has characterised crypto, it's volatility and fluctuation. One of the best ways to navigate this, as I've mentioned many times throughout the book, is to be a contrarian.

When you're a contrarian, you approach crypto investing proactively, rather than reactively. So, when the market is quiet, you go deeper into your research and education. And when the market roars with deafening enthusiasm, you take action in a calm, collected and unemotional way. Allow reason and education to guide your decisions amidst the chaos.

Crypto rewards those who are prepared and ready, but it can be unforgiving to those who are led astray by their impulses and lack of foundational education. It's not about waiting for the perfect moment, it's about seizing the initiative and making each moment count.

So, take the time to learn and empower yourself now. Don't wait for crypto to grab you with fancy headlines and huge gains. Make sure you grab it first and be proactive—instead of reactive.

Chapter 38

When Rules No Longer Apply

On the other side of the great scarcity illusion is abundance, wealth and true freedom.

Now this may be a little controversial, but early in my wealth creation journey I made a crucial observation, and it's one you've no doubt made yourself: the super-rich play by a very different set of rules.

Very wealthy people tend to live beyond the realms and rules of traditional society. They enjoy an extraordinarily different 'reality' to what we normally see. It's a world of lavish holidays, luxury travel experiences, silver service and VIP treatment. A world where dining out isn't just grabbing a meal, it's an exquisite event. Imagine designer homes, luxury sports cars, and magnificent super yachts, and that's just the beginning: self-made charities and foundations, juggling multiple businesses while still having time for personal projects and hobbies, investing in land banks, curating collections of rare items—the list is endless.

But do you want to know something truly exciting? This remarkable way of living is not as far from your reality as it may seem.

You see, crypto has the unparalleled ability to create life-changing, transformative wealth and alter the trajectory of your life, from where you stand now to an abundant reality crafted entirely by you. I've witnessed investors achieve this very transformation within a matter of two to four years. Suddenly, everything I've mentioned above becomes an attainable option within their realm of reality, like it did for me.

At this moment, it may seem like an extravagant fantasy, but this is exactly what can be achieved with education, action and patience. Whether it's your dream to fly around the world first class or retire in an eco-home in the forest, it's entirely within your grasp. Your choices equal your reality. This is the power of this amazing asset class.

So, commit wholeheartedly because crypto will give to you what you give to it. I've experienced it myself. I've done it for my family and friends and I've coached thousands of students worldwide to achieve the same thing.

The treasure trove of wealth awaits. It's abundant, it's available, and it's ready to be claimed by those who commit to pursuing it.

A Final Note: How to Cash In on the Big Opportunity Happening Right Now

As we conclude our journey through the wonderful world of cryptocurrencies, one thing is clear:

The time for action is now.

We stand at the precipice of a financial revolution. The landscape before us shimmers with opportunity and transformative change. This is not just a glimpse of what could be—it's a resounding call to action! Crypto is *the* ground-breaking technology that is poised to redefine our world. We're on the brink of a new financial era—one where the rules are being rewritten, and the possibilities are limitless.

The catalysts for this monumental shift are clear: our traditional financial systems teeter on the edge of collapse, while a new generation, powered by the belief in decentralised finance, is turning away from conventional banks. And the institutional giants of the finance world. One by one they are making their way in. The stage is set for an unprecedented wealth transfer—an opportunity that comes once in a lifetime. This isn't just about investing in a digital asset, it's about participating in a movement that is reshaping the financial landscape for generations to come. Inclusivity, empowerment, and the democratisation of wealth.

The blockchain revolution is sweeping through hundreds of industries—music, supply chain, entertainment, and finance to name a few. It's reshaping the landscape and leaving nothing in its wake. This wave is gaining momentum by the minute, and now is our chance to catch it, rather than sitting on the sidelines and watching it break. Because there's one thing I know for sure:

A major supply shortage is coming.

Wall Street greed *will* power global adoption. This is a fact that can't be denied. It will bring unprecedented buy pressure with it, so we must position ourselves now. Institutions want in, and they will keep coming. But we can get in now, stake our claim and be part of history. We all have a choice: watch from the sidelines and miss the monumental gains or get in the game.

This is the chance to be part of something bigger than ourselves, a chance to level the financial playing field and be part of a global movement for change. The rules of finance and investment are being rewritten as we speak, and the opportunities to redefine our financial future are within reach. The potential for growth in the crypto sphere is boundless, and now is the moment to seize this opportunity and ride the wave all the way to financial freedom.

We get to witness one, maybe two truly incredible feats of innovation and disruption in our lifetime. I believe our next one is already here, and it's called cryptocurrency. An unbelievable transfer of wealth is on its way.

So, the question is, will you be part of it?

Get Started with Digital Wealth Group

I hope you've enjoyed learning about the fascinating and lucrative world of cryptocurrencies, but more importantly, I trust you now know that anyone of any age can profit from this rapidly evolving market.

If you'd like to discover more about this incredible asset class, visit the link below to receive my ninety-minute free training on how to get started today.

Discover How to Profit from This Market and Build A Portfolio You Could Potentially Retire on in Two to Four Years Through Cryptocurrencies.

Watch Now:
www.DigitalWealthGroup.com.au/freetraining

Included are special bonuses, free resources and more!

About Your Author

Sydel Sierra is the co-founder of the Digital Wealth Group. Sydel is passionate about helping people from all walks of life invest in cryptocurrency for maximum returns while minimising risks.

After completing her university degree in physics and mathematics, Sydel's twenties saw her travel, and surround herself with leading entrepreneurs, financial experts and business owners. This was when she first discovered the power of cryptocurrencies, and by the age of thirty, Sydel and her brother were able to retire and live 100% off cryptocurrencies.

Today, Sydel's true passion is helping people create financial sovereignty, particularly during these times with so much geopolitical uncertainty, and believes now more than ever we need to be coming up with a plan B. Sydel lives and breathes crypto and is driven to share her simple and effective strategy to turbocharge a small investment into life-changing gains.

When you work with Sydel, you will learn the best-kept crypto investing secrets to help you rapidly scale and grow your portfolio. She has helped many clients turn five figures to six, seven and eight figures, and cannot wait to help you do the same.

@sydel.sierra

A Message of Gratitude

Thank you to my brother Aden, co-founder of DWG.

Our combined effort and passion allowed us to achieve financial freedom through the power of Cryptocurrencies at such a young age. It was through this medium that we could inspire so many thousands and leave the legacy that is Digital Wealth Group today.

Heartfelt gratitude to the team behind Digital Wealth Group. Through their unwavering dedication and integrity makes all this happen. A special thanks to Jeremy and Michael for being our foundational coaches that helped establish and guide who we are today.

I acknowledge my family for their incredible support and belief.

Our family is founded on the premise of creating a better humanity through self sovereignty, community and financial freedom and this has continued to inspire my message to this day.

I would also like to acknowledge those contrarians who believed in our vision many years ago and gave us a platform, and continue to give us a platform, to share this important message. You are the future makers.

A huge thank you to Rachael Jellick and the entire Kind Press Publishing team for your editorial and support in the process of creating this book.

It has been an honour to work with you all.

Notes

1. Reserve Bank of Australia (2022) *Australian Australian Inflation | Chart Pack, Reserve Bank of Australia*. Available at: https://www.rba.gov.au/chart-pack/aus-inflation.html.

2. Duffin, E. (2022). *U.S. Population by Generation 2019*. [online] Statista. Available at: https://www.statista.com/statistics/797321/us-population-by-generation/#:~:text=Millennials%20were%20the%20largest%20generation.

3. Harper, C. (2019). *Surprise! Millennials Embrace Bitcoin While Boomers, Gen-Xers Hold Traditional Wealth*. [online] Bitcoin Magazine - Bitcoin News, Articles and Expert Insights. Available at: https://bitcoinmagazine.com/markets/surprise-millennials-embrace-bitcoin-boomers-gen-xers-hold-traditional-wealth [Accessed 9 Jan. 2024].

4. Frank, R. (2021). *Millennial Millionaires Plan to Add More Crypto in 2022, CNBC Millionaire Survey Finds*. [online] CNBC. Available at: https://www.cnbc.com/2021/12/16/millennial-millionaires-plan-to-add-more-crypto-in-2022.html?qsearchterm=millionnaires%20crypto [Accessed 9 Jan. 2024].

5. Merchants Getting Ready for Crypto Merchant Adoption of Digital Currency Payments Survey Prepared in Collaboration with PayPal. (n.d.). Available at: https://www2.deloitte.com/content/dam/Deloitte/us/Documents/technology/us-cons-merchant-getting-ready-for-crypto.pdf [Accessed 22 Dec. 2023].

6. Cuthbertson, A. (2021). *The Bitcoin Network Now Handles More Volume than PayPal*. [online] The Independent. Available at: https://www.independent.co.uk/tech/bitcoin-paypal-2021-volume-mastercard-visa-b1964330.html.

7. Anon, (n.d.). *Millennials + money: the Unfiltered Journey*. https://s3-eu-central-1.amazonaws.com/cja-blogassets/wp-content/uploads/sites/3/2016/03/21124209/facebookiq_millennials_money_january2016.pdf.

8. TripleA (2023). *Global Cryptocurrency Ownership Data 2021*. [online] TripleA. Available at: https://triple-a.io/crypto-ownership-data/.

9. Rees, K. (2023). *How Much Bitcoin Is Lost Forever and How Did It Get Lost?* [online] MUO. Available at: https://www.makeuseof.com/how-much-bitcoin-is-lost-forever/#:~:text=Estimates%20suggest%20that%20around%206 [Accessed 9 Jan. 2024].

10. Alternative.me. (2018). Crypto Fear & Greed Index - Bitcoin Sentiment. [online] Available at: https://alternative.me/crypto/fear-and-greed-index/.

11. defillama.com. (n.d.). Chain TVL - DefiLlama. [online] Available at: https://defillama.com/chains.

www.ingramcontent.com/pod-product-compliance
Lightning Source LLC
Chambersburg PA
CBHW022049290426
44109CB00014B/1036